Return ^{to}_{the} Root

"Like a faithful friend, Joyce Rupp accompanies us on a quiet stroll along familiar roads, gently offering us her comfort in small things and revelations in everyday moments. Part poetry, part personal reflection, *Return to the Root* shares her wisdom, which is a light for the journey through our own seasons of life."

Jen Norton
Catholic artist and author of *Surrender All*

"Joyce Rupp uses words to lead us into that place in the soul where there are no words, no sounds—just stillness and peace. Her books never grow old. They always open the ground of our being to something we need to know right now. *Return to the Root* is no exception. It is the most fruitful book I have read this year."

Michael Leach
Author of *Soul Seeing*

"*Return to the Root* is a truly beautiful book, alive with reverence and joy for nature. Each part is full of inspiration for meditation and prayer. I will definitely come back to it again and again!"

Mary Pezzulo
Blogger at *Steel Magnificat* and author of *Stumbling into Grace*

"Joyce Rupp beautifully engages metaphors of creation through her prayers and poetic writing. Wise insights fill the pages of *Return to the Root*, and I am eager to have it guide my reflection in the seasons ahead."

Jessie Bazan
Editor and coauthor of *Dear Joan Chittister*

Return to the Root

reflections on the inner life

JOYCE RUPP

SORIN BOOKS  Notre Dame, IN "in everyday the blessing of weather" by bell hooks from *Appalachian Elegy: Poetry and Place*, copyright © 2012 by Gloria Jean Watkins (bell hooks) and published by University Press of Kentucky. Used with permission of the publisher.

"Ich bin, du Angstlicher . . . /I am, you anxious one" by Rainer Maria Rilke; from *Rilke's Book of Hours: Love Poems to God* by Rainer Maria Rilke, translated by Anita Barrows and Joanna Macy, translation copyright © 1996 by Anita Barrows and Joanna Macy. Used by permission of Riverhead, an imprint of Penguin Publishing Group, a division of Penguin Random House LLC. All rights reserved.

"Japanese Bowl" song by Peter Mayer, copyright 2010, ASCAP. www.petermayer.net.

Scripture quotations are from *New Revised Standard Version Bible*, copyright © 1989 National Council of the Churches of Christ in the United States of America. Used by permission. All rights reserved.

"I Hold My Heart as a Gourd" and "The Garments of God" from *The Selected Poetry of Jessica Powers* and published by ICS Publications, Washington, DC. Copyright Carmelite Monastery, Pewaukee, WI. Used with permission.

---

www.avemariapress.com/sorin-books

Paperback: ISBN-13 978-1-932057-25-6

E-book: ISBN-13 978-1-932057-26-3

Cover image © gettyimages.com.

Cover and text design by Brian C. Conley.

Printed and bound in the United States of America.

Library of Congress Cataloging-in-Publication Data
Names: Rupp, Joyce, author.
Title: Return to the root : reflections on the inner life / Joyce Rupp.
Description: Notre Dame, IN : Sorin Books, [2021] | Includes
    bibliographical references. | Summary: "The author offers meditative,
    uplifting reflections grown out of the seasons, the Church's liturgical
    life, and the small moments that adorn our days that will take readers
    through the year"-- Provided by publisher.
Identifiers: LCCN 2021019357 | ISBN 9781932057256 (paperback) | ISBN
    9781932057263 (ebook)
Subjects: LCSH: Meditations. | BISAC: RELIGION / Christianity / Catholic |
    RELIGION / Spirituality
Classification: LCC BV4832.3 .R87 2021 | DDC 242--dc23
LC record available at https://lccn.loc.gov/2021019357

To my beloved friend Macrina Wiederkehr —
our long years of friendship inspired me
to grow expansive roots in the realm of my inner life.

— and —

To each faithful reader of my monthly newsletters,
for encouragement and assurance
that my writing serves to make a positive difference
in how they go about their lives.

Contents

Introduction

Come to the root of the root of your Self.

~ Jalāl ad-Dīn Rūmī

If you pull up a plant in the garden, dig out a dandelion in the lawn, or find a shrub uprooted by a fierce wind, you will notice that each has a central support system called a taproot from which other smaller roots develop. Trees also start life with this kind of anchoring. Taproots provide stability, nourishment, and growth. When the poet Rumi encourages returning "to the root of the root of your Self," he refers to our spiritual Taproot, the core of our very being, the dwelling place of divinity, the central source of goodness that grounds our existence.

I first came across Rumi's poem in *Living Presence* where the Sufi teacher Kabir Helminski writes about "the essential Self" as an image of wholeness. This includes "divinity, Christ, and the Tao." According to Helminski, this essential Self "is infinite and can never be fully comprehended by consciousness alone—but it is only a partial truth, because at the same time, we can see with the eyes of the essential Self, hear with its ears, act with its will, and forgive with its forgiveness, and love with its love." From my perspective, this essential Self that Rumi encourages us to join consists of the abiding love reflected in the heart of Christ, a divine wisdom residing at the core of every being. I mostly come to know this essential Self through the many forms of goodness that inform my life and shape its identity.

For a long time now I have attended to this presence, this rootedness that sustains my reason for being. Endless work-oriented activity, unwanted disturbances, and a zillion attractive distractions cause me to disregard or forget about this source of love existing at the center of my creatureliness. Even so, time and again I am drawn back to this divine Taproot. This return comes mostly through ordinary events and experiences. Sometimes I am deliberate about awakening and returning to this core of love. At other times I bump into a restored connection without any effort at all.

This book comes from the monthly e-newsletters I've written and shared with readers for a dozen years and have expanded here. The topics surfaced through my experience of daily life. This territory serves repeatedly as a source that moves me to the deeper place inside where the divine Taproot lives, supports, and nurtures my life.

In his letter to the Ephesians, Paul encourages the early Christians to be strengthened in their "inner being" through Christ's Spirit, that they may be "rooted and grounded in love" (Eph 3:16–17). This *inner being, grounded in love,* can be likened to Rumi's imagery of the self held fast by the divine Root. Benedictine monk John Main echoes this thought in *The Way of Unknowing* when he writes about meditation: "We are made free to love *by* Love. . . . We begin to find a wholly new ground to stand on. We discover a rootedness of being which is not just in ourselves, because we find ourselves rooted in God. Rooted in God who is Love. All this happens because we learn the courage to take the attention off of ourselves. We learn to stop thinking about ourselves and to allow ourselves to be. To be still, to be silent, is the lesson and in that stillness and silence we find ourselves in God, in love."

Rootedness and stillness. These twins provide a worthy foundation for spiritual well-being. The content of this book aims to strengthen your inner rootedness, to draw forth that loving nourishment contained in the Taproot of your deepest self. If you allow yourself to be reflective, you can absorb what you read and relate it to your own life experience. In doing this, I am confident you will find yourself returning to the *Root of your root.*

This affinity to one's life is necessary if this book is to make a difference in your life. The wise English mystic Evelyn Underhill recognized and encouraged this relatedness: "We know a thing only by uniting with it; by assimilating it; by an interpenetration of it and ourselves. It gives itself to us, just in so far as we give ourselves to it."

This has been my intent with almost every book I've written. I long for the insights not only to reach into the mind and heart of readers but also to make a difference in how they express their day-to-day life.

I invite you to enter *Return to the Root* with how I concluded my first online newsletter in June 2011. Here is a blessing to wrap around you like the wings of a mother swan enfolding her beloved cygnets within the warmth and shelter of her welcome.

> May you be rooted and grounded in enduring love.
> May you trust this essential core of goodness within you.
> May you choose to be nurtured through times of stillness.
> May this root of divinity strengthen and support you.
> May you discover inner peace to carry you through travails.
> May you return time and again to the Taproot of your life.

Discussion Guide for Small Groups available at www.avemariapress.com/ products/return-to-the-root-discussion-guide.

January

A new year arrives, bringing with it an invitation to cherish life with renewed eagerness. In the northern hemisphere winter reigns, providing an opportunity for interior restoration. This season lures us into the cave of solitude where our relationship to the divine Root is strengthened. Our spiritual growth stretches further in the depths of extended darkness.

Stay, My Heart, Stay

Everything inside of me
longs to flee to where the sun
rinses the winter sky,
filling the day with invitation,

to run where the brilliant light
shines into blushing sunset,
avoiding the space where night
whispers to oncoming darkness.

Do not give in. Stay. Sit inside
the grayness, the airless heart,
day after day after day after day.
Stay and enter the dark void.

Yin space. Lots of it. Cave time.
Pull back a desire for Yang.
Be with the persistent dullness.
Listen intently for the smallest
murmuring of life.

It is there, quiet as an enclosed root
in the seeming dead of winter
secretly sipping from the soil,
waiting for a turn toward warmth,
not giving its strength to worry
or yearning for what is yet to be.

Stay, my heart, stay.
Stay. Stay. Stay where you are.

~ Joyce Rupp

Come to the Root

Just as the plant that is rooted and that we cultivate
is in a constant state of self-transcendence,
leaving behind its former state and being what it is now,
so are we on this journey of spiritual growth.

~ John Main

Come

Every moment of every day the Holy One extends an open invitation to come closer, to connect with the hidden root and imbibe from this lasting relationship. Now is the time to shake off what prevents this visitation. Release what causes stumbling on the path of love and thwarts your ability to reach your truest self. Now is the moment to accept the invitation to be nurtured and transformed by this foundational presence.

to the root

Sink into a quiet space for a restorative time each day. Encourage your roots of love to be strengthened by the divine Taproot. Assimilate the grace-filled nutrients found in the soil of prayer. Breathe deeply and be empowered by this life-giving sustenance so that your fidelity does not topple over in weakness like a tree with a failing root system. As an African proverb wisely states; "When the root is deep, there is no reason to fear the wind."

of the root

Go even deeper in rootedness with the Beloved. Absorb the boundless storehouse of wholeness originating in the divine Taproot. Open all the pores of your spirit. Assimilate these invigorating qualities until their dynamism flows smoothly through your entire being. Become a flourishing plant with an extended root system, a conduit carrying love and goodwill wherever you go. Exhale this effective energy like a healthily-rooted tree breathing oxygen into the lungs of creation.

of your Self

There, at the core of your being—the true Self where the divine and the human meet in undivided kinship—allow yourself to rest in a love too large and unconditional to fully comprehend with the human mind. Set aside egoic demands, nursed grudges, repetitive discouragement, leftover regrets, and stale excuses. Receive this love with the intuitive heart. Become one with the divine Root, a source of restoration for the neglected and famished parts of the soul. Grow ever more fully united with the Root of all love.

Live Life Fully

You are forgetting how to move
to the music of your soul.
You can hardly even hear that inner music
over the clamor of all your obligations.

~ Mirabai Starr

As a gate opens to the new year, three words beckon: *Live life fully.* My aging self urges, "Don't waste a year on the foolishness of needless concern or any attempt to control the uncontrollable. Be attentive to every fragment of joy, each revelation of nature's splendor however small, and to the integrity residing in people who touch your life."

An expression of St. Irenaeus of Lyons has been passed down through the ages: "The glory of God is a human being fully alive." I have cherished that notion of engaging life with enthusiasm. Unfortunately, I have often set this conviction aside, becoming lost in too much work or in absorbing situations requiring acceptance rather than useless worry.

That is why I recommit myself this year to engage as totally as I can with the life I have been given, to use my physical senses—these guests of my body—to welcome and explore what comes my way. When I am in tune with what I see, hear, taste, touch, and smell, an amazing amount of joy comes into view. This is when I can honestly say, "I love life."

I also recommit to relishing my mind and cherishing my spirit, to pause instead of push, to draw back and take a second look instead of crashing automatically into the jungle of activity. When I allow myself to be deliberately alert to what is in the present, I establish an awakened receptivity, an increased ability to stay grounded in my core integrity.

Recommitment to living fully fires up the rusty spark plugs of my attitude. It changes the let's-just-get-it-done approach into one of there's-so-much-to-discover-and-enjoy. Then I am able to start the engines of my work with eager enthusiasm instead of poky resignation.

After thirty-seven-year-old brain scientist Jill Bolte Taylor recovered from an initially debilitating stroke, she reflected on her experience in *My Stroke of Insight*: "I view the garden in my mind as a sacred patch of cosmic real estate that the universe has entrusted to me to tend over the years of my lifetime." After I read Taylor's book, I pondered what I had done with the brain entrusted to me for a lifetime. This led me to gratitude for what this part of my physical self is able to do. Before this reflection, I took for granted that my brain worked. Now, I marvel at being able to think, make choices and decisions, investigate and be intrigued with fresh information, and make connections that come together in a way that brings purpose and meaning. And how wonderful it is that my brain automatically knows what to do with the 86 billion neurons stored in my body, how it keeps everything functioning as intended.

The Indian poet Rabindranath Tagore believed that "a stream of life" ran through his veins and that this flow of life resonated throughout all of creation. Whenever I read Tagore's poems and essays I marvel at how he fully engaged with life. In a letter to a friend at year's end, Tagore wrote:

> The year '99 would never come twice in my life. . . . I often think how each day a new day dawns—some steeped in hues of the rising or setting sun . . . the shimmering blue of reflecting clouds; some cheerful-like white flowers in the light of the full moon—how very fortunate I am! . . . When I ponder over this possibility, a desire grows in me to look closely at the world again: to consciously greet each sunrise in my life and say goodbye to each sunset like I would to a good friend. . . . Why can't I gather all those enchanting days and nights that are vanishing from my life . . . this

> peace and grace filling up the empty spaces between heav-
> en and earth . . . ?

Sometimes we only awaken to the fullness of our life when we experience a severe loss—a part of our physical self, such as eyesight;
the devastation of a basic material necessity; some part of the natural environment we've treasured; or the havoc wreaked in a human
relationship. One year I was rendered speechless. Literally. A week
before a conference where I was scheduled to speak all day, I could
not utter a word. A sinus infection had led to a severe case of lar-
yngitis. My physician warned, "Don't use your voice. Save it for the
conference. Do not even whisper." All week long I kept still. It was
only when I lost my ability to speak that I recognized the preciousness of having a voice. On each day of my body's imposed silence
I thought of how I had never given a second thought to possessing
that precious gift of being able to speak.

On the other hand, when we have learned to live with zest, to
experience life with a wide-open attentiveness, we can continue to
live this way even during our final days of life. I often marveled
at my friend Jeanne's vibrant spirit. She radiated an eagerness to
be involved and learn from whatever she could. When Jeanne was
nearing her death, she smiled at me and whispered how much joy
she found in listening to the first birdsong at dawn. I thought, *Even
now she is greeting what enlivens her spirit.*

But why wait for loss or misfortune to rouse us from our lethar-
gy? Let's not lose something in order for us to appreciate it. We can
start to live more fully by listening, *really listening,* to both our interi-
or and exterior world. As philosopher and nature writer Kathleen
Dean Moore states in *Holdfast,* "*We must love life before loving its meaning,*
as Dostoyevsky told us. We must love life, and some meaning may
grow from that love. But *if love of life disappears, no meaning can console
us.*"

This new year beckons us to be persons fully alive with the glory
of divinity. Are we ready to love life and step wholeheartedly into
what awaits us?

My Last Day

This day is a gift. Do not waste a single moment.

~ **Nancy Wood**

A blip in the expanding universe,
a wink of the awakened eye,
a thin wisp of passing cloud,
one in-breath, one out-breath.

The sojourn on this planet,
whether a day or ninety years,
quick as a lizard's tongue
we're here, we're gone.

But, oh, if that brief piece of life
ripens with kindheartedness,
this momentary stay becomes
a transforming, enduring light.

To live each passing day as if the last,
to place each trouble in perspective,
to bow to what seeks more acceptance,
to stretch toward what love requests.

Inquisitive, open, tender, grateful,
united as kin with pebble and partridge,
embracing the gift of human encounters,
cherishing every touch of the soul.

~ **Joyce Rupp**

Worthwhile Resolutions

It takes effort to direct thoughts to things
that are true, honorable, just, pure, lovely,
gracious, worthy of praise.

~ Amy Kuebelbeck

No matter how life is currently unfolding, I always look forward to greeting a new year. Its open space appears inviting, and the fresh prospects instill hope. Each January presents an opportunity to reestablish and reclaim what promises to keep me balanced and growing.

In late December, a television newscaster disparaged New Year's resolutions as worthless, probably because studies show that almost 80 percent of them will be broken or discarded before the month is over. In spite of this fact, I believe resolutions to be valuable for my personal growth. Through the years I've found an intentional focus on some aspect of my attitude and behavior to be of substantial value. One simple intention can make a big difference in how I live.

I prefer to call these resolutions "affirmations," positive intentions to guide and grow my life into greater wholeness. These simple statements in the present tense remind me that not only are there more changes for me to make, but also that making these changes is possible. Of course, the affirmation has to be practical and doable. If I expect a complete makeover of who I am in one year, I will surely be disappointed. I also need to hold the vision near to my heart each day. That's the key. Write the resolution down, read and renew the intention each morning, and then make an effort to practice it. In doing so, the desired change imperceptibly takes hold as the year proceeds and gradually becomes internalized.

I never have to look far for what might be nudging me toward transformation. In the past, these have been some of my affirmations: be aware of the good in my life that I take for granted, give sufficient time for leisure and less time to endless tasks, close the day with a prayer of gratitude for something beneficial that took place, and cease holding grudges toward those who offend me. Sometimes these affirmations have been repeated in future years due to my weak efforts, but usually my life reveals definite growth because of them.

This year my intention to change arrived in a four-day end-of-year meditation retreat. Each day found me sitting next to the same person as we moved through many periods of silence. The first two days went well. But in the morning of the third an irritating noise announced my wake-up call. It came in the form of a continual sniffle.

On my right sat a hefty man in his forties. As soon as we began the early morning meditation he began to sniff loudly. *Surely he'll pull out a tissue and blow his nose*, I thought. *Doesn't he realize how obnoxious that sounds?* But the sniffling went on and on. *I think I'll count how often he sniffs. I'll bet it's every minute.* Sure enough, about every fifty seconds came another big, wet one. Finally, I became conscious of what was going on inside of me. I smiled at how I was allowing myself to be distracted by Mr. Sniffles' behavior.

After all this interior fussing, I finally did what wise teachers of meditation suggest: I chose to let the sound be there. Before long the sniffle became just so much white noise. My irritated self settled into stillness. This taught me anew that I can choose to let negativity rule my response to what I do not want, or I can choose to simply allow it to be present. The days will rarely fail to bring something I do not desire or someone whose personality traits or behavior I'd like to adjust or eliminate, whether those of a familiar person or a stranger I encounter. Instead of focusing on these frustrations, my affirmation for this year includes, "I am at peace with what I cannot change."

After I shared this experience regarding my accepting the irritating behavior of another, I learned about a husband who "snores in varying decibel levels," another who talks way too much, and "a woman who sits behind me at church who really rattles my cage."

The comment that especially captured my attention was from a friend who wrote, "I had a similar experience. I became obsessed with a woman at a retreat who was a fussy eater and held up the buffet line every meal. I let her drive me nuts for a few days; I always seemed to end up eating where she was sitting and was totally obsessed with her rudeness. I finally calmed down and began to realize she was to be my teacher. I always smile when I reflect on that week. Do you suppose the leaders plug in those sorts of people at meditation retreats for slow learners like me?"

To begin this new year, I've taken a few verses from Psalm 139 and adapted them to fit my focus of renewal. Perhaps you may find these verses beneficial when you look at how you intend to live in this new year.

> Holy One, you created me in my mother's womb.
> You know the core goodness residing within me.
> You also know my propensity for self-orientation.
> You see how I want others to meet my expectations.
> You know the thoughts and feelings that run rampant
> when I encounter someone whose behavior I resist.
> If I say, "Surely I can get this person to be as I want,"
> nudge me with your grace-filled message:
> "Leave the other person's transformation alone.
> Tend to your own shortcomings that have to change."
> In this new year, guide me to a clearer awareness.
> Lead me to move beyond a wish to modify others.
> Focus my attention on how to approach what I resist.
> May I become more alert and accepting of the reality
> that the only person I am able to change is myself.

Stretching

Change can never take place if we don't get out
of our comfort zones and our old patterns.
We have to learn to stretch ourselves beyond
our limited prospective and to look at our definition
of truth with a brand-new eye.

~ Sobonfu Somé

One word keeps popping up when I think about my approach to the coming year: *stretch*. This simple word seems to be inviting me into another twelve months of growth. A year ago a friend introduced me to *Classical Stretch*, a fitness program intended to "rebalance bodies, keep joints healthy and pain-free, increase flexibility and release muscle tension, improve posture and range of motion." That is quite a project to accomplish. I have learned that none of this can happen without concentration and the discipline that physical "stretching" requires. I can't just hope to have it happen. I have to actively give myself to it by being involved in the process.

The results of *Classical Stretch* can be applied as metaphors for the interior stretching that also enables me to stay fit in the spiritual sphere of life. With that in mind, I hope to be attentive to the following:

I stretch outward . . . to the magnificent cosmos, a reminder of mystery, wonder, and the vast expanse of creation. I rebalance my perspective in the light of this cosmic view and gain a wider vision in which my problems and passing frustrations take their proper place in proportion to what occurs in the larger world.

I stretch inward . . . to where my spiritual strength and source of inspiration resides. I improve my inner flexibility by lessening the strain and stress of trying to manage everything on my own by rec-ognizing a power much greater than myself that I can rely on for guidance.

I stretch around . . . to suffering people who exist both near and far. I improve my range of compassionate motion by increasing an awareness of distress in the world. The further I stretch the more my intention grows to act on behalf of those in need and do what I can to lessen their pain.

I stretch away from . . . my instinctual urge to always be right, to take sides, fight back, mock, or treat as an adversary anyone whose ideas and way of life differ significantly from mine. I improve this part of my inner posture by practicing nonjudgment and nurturing peace of mind and heart.

I stretch toward . . . a hope that refuses to be obliterated by the turbulence and disjointedness submerging society in division and discord. I release tension in my spiritual muscles by seeking kinship with others who have made it through difficult times and who trust in better days to come.

I stretch beyond . . . anything that keeps me from being at home with the Holy One and with other persons. I reach out with a gen-erous love that oils the loving joints of relationship. I keep these connections strong by the spiritual vitamins of daily prayer and the decision to forego self-centeredness.

I stretch in all these directions. As I do so, I reinforce what is vital for my spiritual well-being.

A Winter Prayer: Strengthening Darkness

I have learned things in the dark that I could never have learned in the light, things that have saved my life over and over again, so that there is really only one logical conclusion. I need darkness as much as I need light.

~ Barbara Brown Taylor

The extensive darkness in winter especially affects certain people who suffer from seasonal affective disorder, resulting in depression due to the deprivation of light. It is understandable that darkness might be viewed as an enemy. But darkness can also be a friend. Velma Frye sings of this positive aspect in a song based on Macrina Wiederkehr's phrase in *Seven Sacred Pauses*: "O beautiful darkness, O comforting darkness." How can darkness bring comfort? Think of a child in the lightless womb, a shade tree on a beastly-hot summer day, the midnight sky revealing a star-studded cosmos, the ease of sleep in a darkened room.

Winter is the season of nature's restoration and renewal. This barren period actually strengthens the world of nature during long hours of darkness. Less light allows for a quiet resting of the land, vegetation, and creatures. What is quite amazing is that trees are already budding in wintertime. If you look closely at the terminal buds found at the ends of branches, you won't see the future life within their tight protection, but it is hiding there. These buds are storing up energy that will enable them to open with warming sun and spring rain.

In the following prayer, I name the Holy One as our Strengthening Darkness, a presence of repose and restoration for when we need interior reinforcement.

O Strengthening Darkness, I trust you are with me in the dormant, winter seasons of my spirit.

Each morning when I awaken with light still hiding in the sleeve of winter's night, I turn to you to receive assistance to meet the challenging requirements of the day.

Like terminal buds drawing strength from the roots of a wintered tree, I greet the darkest days of the year with confidence, trusting that the potency of your love will boost my resilience and strengthen my courage.

During this season when the hours of daylight are shortened, I remember the radiance of your divine light within me. The glistening stars in the darkened sky assure me of your presence even when I do not sense your nearness.

Winter darkness invites me to breathe in stillness, to rest in the arms of your silence. In this receptive posture you can deepen and enhance what is of greatest value within my spirit.

Strengthening Darkness, I am like the terminal buds on the tree of life, patiently waiting, trusting that my spiritual vitality is being reinforced during this dark season of rest. May these valued movements of the heart bolster my faith when I find life to be uncertain and ambiguous. Teach me to trust that darkness can be a source of growth. I will wait patiently until whatever seems buried in my spirit's wintry repose awakens and unfurls with fortified stamina.

February

Love, love, love. In the middle of this month, the celebration of Valentine's Day reminds us what love involves: appreciation of the human spirit's capacity for an immense amount of kindness, faithfulness, and unselfish giving. We choose to participate in loving movements of the heart, such as understanding, forgiveness, graciousness, and vulnerability.

Love Received, Love Released

They gather 'round in memory,
these loves of mine through the years,
some tarnished and rusty with wear,
others durable as a circle of gold.

Where would I be, who would I be,
without their support, their belief
in my abilities, their forgiveness?
I marvel at the kindness and care
of these beloveds, generously
imprinting their love on my heart
and choosing to stay.

Today snowflakes are falling gently,
caressing the February landscape.
I sit holding memories of being loved
and loving, covered with a gratitude,
lasting much longer than a snowfall,
restoring a desire to generate love,
to give as much as I have received.

~ Joyce Rupp

Love Generously

Mary took a pound of costly perfume made of pure
nard, anointed Jesus' feet, and wiped them with her
hair. The house was filled with the fragrance of the
perfume.

~ **John 12:3**

Each of the four Christian gospels presents some version of the
anointing of Jesus. In Luke's story a woman in the city washes the
feet of Jesus with her flood of tears, then anoints and dries them
with her hair. Matthew depicts Jesus at the house of Simon the lep-
er, where an unnamed woman enters with expensive ointment and
pours it over the head of Jesus. Mark also has this unnamed woman
at Simon's house but adds more details: the ointment is nard in an
alabaster jar. John's description of this scene most catches my attention because he identifies the woman who anoints Jesus as Mary
from Bethany. The naming of this close friend lets me know that a
gesture of devotion took place. When John also mentions that a sen-
suous fragrance filled the house, this piece of information suggests
the depth and quality of Mary's generous love.

All the versions of this story contain two related features: a woman anoints, and she does so liberally, whether with tears or expensive
oil. There is no holding back in regard to either abundance or price.
Each woman pours the oil or tears on Jesus, either upon his head or
his feet. As they do so, their focus rests directly and completely on the
one whom they are anointing, rather than pointing to themselves.

What motivates this expansive giving? Each woman had her own
personal relationship with Jesus, but it would seem that with this magnanimous and humble outpouring of love all four acknowledged a

comparable movement in their hearts: immense respect, rapt affection, and a profound appreciation for how Jesus touched their lives. Each one wanted to demonstrate how much she loved him.

Did these women expect anything in return from Jesus? It seems not. There is no indication of "I'll love you if" or "I'll love you when" in their actions. Instead of these conditions which block self-giving love, each story points to this: "I'll demonstrate my love for you. I'll take the risk to let you know this." With that intention tears cascade or an alabaster jar tilts and a movement of love comes pouring forth, an offering graciously received by Jesus.

This pouring forth of love is an act of faith, the kind of risk-taking that novelist Paulo Coelho shares in *The Spy* when he muses on the Greek myth of Eros, the god of love, and Psyche, who becomes his queen. Eros asks just one thing of Psyche: that she never see his face, a sign that she trusts him fully. Curiosity overcomes the young queen, and she disobeys that request. In doing so, she returns to her old self and has to leave the palace. Coelho comments, "Love is an act of faith and its face should always be covered in mystery. Every moment should be lived with feeling and emotion because if we try to decipher it and understand it, the magic disappears. . . . We trust in the hand that leads us. If we do not allow ourselves to be frightened, we will always awaken in a palace; if we fear the steps that will be required by love and want it to reveal everything to us, the result is that we will be left with nothing."

All four women who anointed Jesus trusted in the love that led them. They went beyond reluctance and fear and entered into mystery, unsure of the outcome of their gestures of devotion. Each one approached Jesus with faith that she would be safe with him as she expressed her gratitude.

The alabaster jar of costly nard serves as a metaphor for our own giving from the fullness of our heart. The beauty of these gospel stories teaches that real love goes beyond hesitation, trepidation, and self-consciousness. We offer this gift of love without expectation of something in return because, as quantum chemist Michelle Francl-Donnay reminds us, "we were all fashioned to be generous."

The ointment poured on Jesus is "costly." Loving generously does not come without a cost. Love often has a price tag. It requires something of us, whether that be sharing our prized personal time, our vulnerability, or a willingness to love despite not being thanked or receiving love in return. How well I recall a beloved aunt of mine who developed Alzheimer's. One of her adult children visited my aunt faithfully even though my aunt no longer recognized her. Another one of my aunt's children never went to visit, using the excuse, "Mom doesn't know me, anyhow. And it's too painful to see her that way." The first child brought the costly ointment of love to her visit. The second held onto the costly gift and never shared it.

When the pouring forth of our love challenges us to hesitate, we might look at our intention or motivation. Is the action we are about to take mainly for self satisfaction, a sense of success, or furthering the need for affirmation? Is the giving of love to assuage some guilt? Is pouring the ointment of our love done openheartedly, with no resentment or regret? Can we trust that the outpouring of our heart's precious ointment serves a larger purpose, one that might not be recognized?

When we love generously, sometimes gifts we are initially unaware of hide within the gesture. While each woman's outpouring of love upon Jesus seems to have held only the motivation of expressing genuine devotion, each one of them undoubtedly received something in return: the pleasure of following her heart's unselfish instinct; finding enough courage to reach beyond fear and self-doubt; being able to let go of what others thought (such as the disciples who protested about the nard being too expensive). Most surely, each woman felt a resonant joy by giving in such full measure.

The "costly perfume made of pure nard" that Mary used to anoint Jesus contained such intensity that the wafting scent floated through the entire house. Like that aromatic oil, pure love has no bounds. The more profuse this love, the further it spreads and the longer-lasting its effect. Like Mary's anointing, the fragrance of our love-filled heart has the potential to reach far beyond ourselves.

Fertile Seeds of Kindness

"It is easy to sympathize at a distance,"
said an old gentleman with a beard.
"I value more the kind word
that is spoken close to my ear."

~ E. M. Forster

An astonishing gift of kindness landed on my doorstep one February afternoon. Imagine my wonderment when I opened the front door to retrieve my mail and found beside the mailbox a tall container consisting of four mailing tubes, each twenty-four inches in length, neatly taped together to form one long cylinder. "What on earth can this be?" I wondered as I lifted the long item and carried it inside the house.

As I unwrapped the painstakingly put together mailing tube, I pulled forth the content and let out a gasp. There it was—a magnificent walking stick. Included with it was a lovely note from a Texan, letting me know he was in his late eighties and grateful for having read some of my publications. This man, whom I'd never met, described the cactus from which the walking stick was made: "I came upon this plant all by itself, crying 'find me a home.'" He then decided to create a hardy brown and beige walking stick for me.

As I stood with the walking stick in my hand, the words "generosity, patience, and care" surfaced. Each one attached itself to the word "kindness" as I thought about the unexpected gift. Not only did the reception of the walking stick prompt joy, it resurrected my awareness of how one touch of kindness from another person births our desire to be more thoughtful and considerate.

Another incident of kindness living in my memory reminds me of how the Spirit of Love draws us to bring comfort to another. Several years ago I stayed at a lovely cottage in the woods not far beyond the Rivendell retreat center on Bowen Island in British Columbia. Due to the large number of retreatants, the event was held in the town at the bottom of the winding, steep hill. The rain never stopped pouring that entire day, which made my weariness feel especially heavy at 8 p.m. when I returned to the retreat center.

As I started to trudge up the gravel slope in the thick darkness to go home to the cottage, I remembered I had not left the porch light on. I resigned myself to walk carefully as I found my way in the steady rain. But as I drew halfway near the cottage my heart soared with joy—the house was glowing. Someone had turned all the lights on. I instantly felt sheltered and welcomed. But that was not all. As I entered and went into the living room, I found a vase of fresh flowers and a handwritten note on the table before the fireplace. Marks, one of the hosts, had written, "Welcome, Joyce. The fire has been laid." I felt such warmth from that thoughtful, gracious gesture.

To this day the memory of that kindness kindles my heart with warm gratitude and influences my desire to be hospitable. That is often the effect an unexpected gesture of goodwill can have—the desire to carry the good deed forward. In *A Book of Wonders*, Edward Hays uses the metaphor of watermelon seeds to describe this generativity: "A watermelon produces a thousand good works!" This Islamic saying originated when watermelons were mostly eaten out-of-doors, so their seeds dropped to the ground to become the source of countless new watermelon plants. While appearing to be an innocent folk proverb, this Islamic saying about watermelons contains superior spiritual advice. Our good works, like watermelons, also contain seeds, invisible yet richly fertile with potential for more good. Watermelon wisdom says to be lavishly careless in doing good deeds so that the tiny invisible seeds within your works will be generously scattered everywhere.

Fertile seeds of kindness strewn in our lives have long-lasting consequences when they awaken an awareness within us to do likewise. That's the beauty about this golden virtue. Someone's thoughtful deed contains more than just the action itself. "Kindness leaves a repository of goodness," writes E. Jane Rutter in *Give Us This Day*. "Surely, acts of kindness are seeds planted by the Holy Spirit to awaken us to the goodness inherent in one another." Such was the sunny winter day when I was ready to walk out the door of my apartment building and noticed the handwritten sign: "Be careful. Very icy sidewalk." Had it not been for that sign, I surely would have fallen and perhaps broken a limb. As I walked to my car, I resolved to be more considerate, more like the person who cared enough to write the note.

I never tire of being amazed at the presence of kindness. Perhaps that's due to living in an age when world news includes vast amounts of humanity's unkindness. Each day I read or hear about the harsh and violent way people treat one another. Yet, if I look for kind deeds, I'll find that my world has an abundance of these, too. A good portion of kindness goes by unnoticed. Maybe these actions are taken for granted, such as an all-night vigil with a sick child that allows the other parent to rest and the child to feel safe. Sometimes a worthy act of love is entirely within the heart so that the kindness is imperceptible, such as choosing to not point out the faults of another when an argument ensues.

In a way, kindness is like a little miracle. We go about our day expecting it to be quite ordinary and then someone's thoughtfulness touches us with comfort, assistance, needed joy, assurance, laughter, hope-filled insight, or some other form of blessedness. When I am alert enough to receive or extend this miracle of love, I am always the better for it.

Lean on Me

God also holds us . . . and longs to comfort and reassure us. But often we are so bruised and afraid we find it hard to trust, to relax, to allow God to cradle and carry us.

~ Edwina Gateley

Several weeks ago at the eucharistic liturgy I sat directly behind an older couple caring for a child whom I presumed to be their granddaughter. For the first fifteen minutes of the liturgy the girl played with items in a canvas bag filled with books and toys. Then she turned her body toward the grandmother. She leaned against the older woman's thick arm and laid her head against it, much like a kitten in want of attention brushing up against its owner's leg. With the ease of someone much practiced in knowing the secret message, the older woman quietly opened her arm and drew the child onto her lap. Once the child was situated there, she curled up with her legs dangling far over the side of grandmother's wide lap. The girl rested comfortably there, abandoning herself in complete trust. She soon fell asleep and remained that way until the conclusion of the liturgy.

I kept being drawn to gaze upon the older woman and the gangly-limbed child, sensing something within that scene calling me inward. Gradually I realized what captured my attention. There before me was an image of the divine Mother. Actually, it was more than an image. I sensed this sacred presence in the loving way the grandmother received the child.

I thought, *This is how I am held in the arms of divine love.* That realization brought an inner smile. Then I thought of all those gathered in the church, each one being held in a similar manner, whether they recognized it or not. *If only they were conscious of this*, I mused, *what a difference it would make in how they experience the difficult things in life. If only each of us could remember this love on the days when we are weary, troubled, ill, or out of sorts. If only we took time to pause and let ourselves be held on the lap of the Great Mother and rest there.*

A different sense of being held in divine love came at another church shortly after witnessing the grandmother and child. I joined a multitude of kindred spirits at First Christian Church intent on solidarity with those affected by a terrorist attack in New Zealand. The event included speakers from diverse religions and ethnicities. Each man and woman spoke of the need to be actively engaged in bringing an end to the hatred and violence prompted by racial and religious bigotry. The gathering was subdued until Rabbi David Kaufman spoke and led us into a deeper sphere of unity. He encouraged us to believe in the strength that comes from standing with others in their pain. Then he began to sing Bill Withers' well-known song, "Lean on Me." After the first line, all of us instantly joined in singing the entire song with him. By the time we reached the last line, I felt an amazing surge of compassion and hope moving among us. At that moment, I think everyone in the church wanted to do whatever they could to be a person that someone suffering could lean on. No one said it out loud, but I'm confident we each felt we could be the arms of the Holy, welcoming anyone who needed holding when they were hurting.

If only we could keep moments like that alive in us as we move through our ordinary days. For it is there, where we live, that we will encounter people who long for someone to lean on. They may not speak their need out loud or let on that they're hurting, so we have to stay awake and watch for where our presence could be a source of comfort.

This need for alertness is apparent in the garden of Gethsemane where Jesus went to pray before he was led away to his death. At that fateful moment, how much Jesus must have yearned for loving arms to wrap around him. In his need for support, he rose and went to the disciples, explaining how he was "deeply grieved." One can almost hear Jesus begging for them to "stay awake," to be there with him. Instead, the disciples fall asleep and leave him alone to bear his agony. Jesus has no one to lean on, no lap to lay his head on when terror overcomes him. What angst accompanies his question, "Could you not stay awake with me one hour?" (Mt 26:40). "Could you not let me lean on you?"

The experience of Jesus with those who failed to be there for him continues today in suffering people who have no one to support them during their most difficult times. These people live in our families, belong to our parishes and religious communities, work beside us, and dwell in our neighborhoods. Our personal care, understanding, empathy, and prayer can uphold them when they have life-threatening surgery, struggle to overcome addictions, live with a stark depression, wrestle with financial troubles, or develop other situations with troubling consequences. Homeless individuals; immigrant families with no one as their advocate; persons scorned for religious beliefs, ethnicity, or sexual orientation—the suffering of these persons could ease if they had someone to support them.

Will we be the welcoming place for others to lean their heart? Will we do what we can to lessen the agony of those who suffer in their Gethsemanes? Will we permit others to be a supportive presence for us when we are hurting? Will we take our pain to the divine Beloved and allow ourselves to be held in that reassuring embrace?

Willing to Be Vulnerable

It may be only in our vulnerability,
in our actually *being* wounded,
that love gains its full power.

~ **Gerald G. May**

Hiking animates my spirit, whether on a trail leading to some place I've not been or to a favorite site. Thus my eagerness to set foot on a path to the Fifth Falls in Gooseberry Park, a scenic route above the north shore of Lake Superior in Minnesota. A friend I had not been with for many years accompanied me that day. Barbara described walking in national parks previously so I assumed she was familiar with hiking.

Not so. I soon learned that her hikes were mainly on smooth concrete. When we met our first of many exposed roots, mud puddles, and a steady uphill climb with many patches of good sized rocks, I heard a distinctive pause behind me. I turned around and noticed Barbara's concern about moving on. We went a little further and she again stopped. This time when I turned I noticed the bottom of her shoes lacked the required treads. I reached out instinctively and offered my hand to her. She quickly accepted and we continued on, making it to a bridge at the top of the trail where we rejoiced in reaching the turning point.

That evening I thought about our time on the trail. Barbara believed she learned something from me about hiking, but actually, I was the student—becoming more aware of what it means to be vulnerable from Barbara's risk-taking, courage, trust, humility, and most of all, her willingness to receive from another. We could have turned back and discontinued the hike, but she accepted my outstretched hand, acknowledging she couldn't walk safely by herself. Barbara's trust reminded me of how much we need one another's companionship to go beyond the obstacles blocking our way, if only we will receive that assistance.

David Whyte assures his readers that "vulnerability is not a weakness, a passing indisposition, or something we can arrange to do without. Vulnerability is not a choice. Vulnerability is the underlying, ever present and abiding undercurrent of our natural state. To run from vulnerability is to run from the essence of our nature. . . . in refusing our vulnerability we refuse the help needed at every turn of our existence." As an American, being vulnerable challenges me because I live in a culture where individualism ranks high on the list of admirable qualities. Impoverished people who require aid regarding life's necessities are viewed as lazy by some persons who have plenty. Our culture deems it commendable to "pull yourself up by your own bootstraps," to be strong, tough it out, be as independent as possible, and avoid needing help. Questions also abound in relation to being vulnerable: Isn't it risky to give one's self too fully in trust to another? Don't people suffer from betrayals? Haven't we heard about the nasty scammers and opportunists who take advantage of those who inadvertently enlist in rip-offs?

In spite of this, I have come to value vulnerability and its effect on my personal growth. Choosing to rely on another for support, accepting help when it's offered, trusting in the durability of caring relationships—these decisions might be difficult, but they are absolutely essential for love to take hold in my heart.

In my mid-twenties, I came across C. S. Lewis's book *The Four* •
Loves, in which he names these four types as Philia (friendship), Caritas (love of everyone), Eros (passion, erotic love), and Agape (love of God). Lewis insists that "to love at all is to be vulnerable. Love anything and your heart will be wrung and possibly broken. If you want to make sure of keeping it intact you must give it to no one, not even an animal. Wrap it carefully round with hobbies and little luxuries; avoid all entanglements. Lock it up safe in the casket or coffin of your selfishness. But in that casket, safe, dark, motionless,

airless, it will change. It will not be broken; it will become unbreak-able, impenetrable, irredeemable."

These insights opened a bolted door inside me and transformed the way I relate to others. The above quote, in particular, confront-ed my vacillation about entering into enduring friendships. In ear-ly adulthood, I fearfully held my affections firmly inside a heavily guarded heart. I had not yet learned that any true relationship re-quires being open and the humble honesty of allowing myself to be seen for who I am—both the polished and the tarnished dimen-sions—and the acceptance of sometimes feeling dependent, weak, and not fully in control.

Without loving and being loved, without choosing to be vulnera-ble and to trust, the heart becomes limited in its capacity to establish a significant bond with others. A person may have very few material possessions, experience agonizing medical issues, or be deluged in unresolved problems but if love is accompanied by vulnerability, the most difficult experiences can be endured.

In *Almost Everything,* Anne Lamott writes, "Love has bridged the high-rises of despair we were about to fall between. Love has been a penlight in the blackest, bleakest nights. Love has been a wild an-imal, a poultice, a dinghy, a coat. Love is why we have hope. . . . 'God is love,' we Christians like to remind ourselves, and every act of love highlights God in the world, because love is not just an idea. Love is something alive, living, personal, and true, the creating and nourishing power within life."

Companies everywhere are broadcasting this month's celebra-tion of Valentine's Day with advertisements to buy and give flowers, stuffed animals, candy, jewelry, and all sorts of things to show one's love. All this, however, is a momentary sign of affection. What truly counts is to be there for another in both the good and not-so-good times, to be ready to both give and receive from one another.

Please Forgive Me

You can't forgive without loving.
And I don't mean sentimentality.
I don't mean mush. I mean having
enough courage to stand up and say,
"I forgive. I'm finished with it."

~ Maya Angelou

An unexpected letter startled and inspired me. It came from some-one I worked with almost forty years ago. Neither of us had corre-sponded or been in touch since then. With puzzlement, I took in the message she asked me to receive: "Please forgive me. I forgive you." I reached back in memory to try to recall what situation or behavior had precipitated needing forgiveness on either of our parts. All I could remember is that we did not like each other. But I could not locate any memorable residue of hurt or recognizable discord in myself.

There I sat with the letter in my hands, marveling at her humility and openness in writing what she did. I felt I had nothing for which to forgive. Would I respond? And if so, how? Then, a memory sur-faced of an incident from my past. About fifteen years ago I was leading a retreat at a church where I ministered years earlier. During the break, a tall, thin man entered the room and came over to me. I recognized him as the friendly mail-carrier from that era. He stood before me and briefly reintroduced himself before plunging into his request, "I've been in a program for recovering alcoholics. I'm here to ask your forgiveness for a terrible comment I made to you one day when I delivered your mail."

My first response was to object, "I have no idea what you said to me, and I most certainly have never held anything against you." But I did not say that. Instead, I looked into his sorrowing eyes and assured him that I did, indeed, forgive him with all my heart. Such a look of relief passed over his face. The tears in his eyes told me so much. Immediately after his thank you he fled the building, obviously too overwhelmed with relief and embarrassment to remain.

Back to the letter I received. I do not know what led the sender to ask for my forgiveness and to assure me of hers. I only knew she merited a forgiveness response from me so that she could go on peacefully with her life. I wanted her to feel the freedom of having the clouded space cleared in her soul. I also wanted to be sure no leftover, shadowy dislike remained in my own.

A few days later, I sat down with her letter alongside some of the gospel stories. There I found Jesus asking that those who criminalized and crucified him be forgiven, and later his gracious pardon of the disciples who had hurled his love aside with their denial, betrayal, and abandonment. This meditation led me to write my response to the letter I had received. I expressed gratitude for her courage and vulnerability and offered assurance of complete forgiveness of any past hurt. I also requested her forgiveness for anything I had done to cause her to feel offended or rejected. While I struggled to find the appropriate words, after the letter was written and sent, I felt a clarity in my spirit.

The forgiveness asked of me in that letter is minuscule compared with the mountain-sized wounds caused by people who eventually speak their sorrow and ask pardon for such things as perpetrating physical and sexual abuse, ruining a reputation, destroying a marriage, obliterating a child's self-esteem, emptying a bank account, killing another person while driving drunk, and other seemingly unforgiveable actions. And yet, there are those who find it in their hearts to respond with "I forgive you."

Rabbi Rami Shapiro wisely contends that "forgiveness is not forgetting, excusing, accepting, denying, or numbing yourself to pain. If someone hurts you, it is unreasonable to think that you can just forget it and move on. Forgetting is not a matter of will. You cannot forget on command. Neither can you will yourself not to feel hurt when a hurtful act is recalled. Nor would it be wise to do so." And then Shapiro names how relief and peace become possible: "Forgiveness is letting go. Letting go means that you do not cling to memories and feelings." In the process of forgiving and letting go, courage and compassion wind their way through our pain and eventually rise to the surface. These assistants to forgiveness act in us to free the wrongdoer and us from the wound that held us captive.

If there is a list of the "Ten Most Difficult Things for Humans to Do," asking for forgiveness and offering it are probably at the top. Why is forgiveness such a seemingly impossible gesture? Why do the old, sharp pieces of personal injury keep poking at us, no matter how we try to dull their edges? It comes down to being willing to stop "picking at the sore," as one reader described it. We do that every time the memories and feelings surge and we acknowledge their arrival but do not invite them to stay by constantly dredging up how the hurt happened or by dwelling on thoughts of revenge.

Jack Kornfield writes in *A Path with Heart*, "Forgiveness is an easing of your own heart and an acknowledgement that, no matter how strongly you may . . . have suffered . . . , you will not put another person out of your heart." That's what I believe I was being asked to do with the letter I received—to reassure the sender she had a place in my heart. And she does.

Enticing My Heart

O Ancient Love,
forever enticing my heart
into a complete acceptance
of belonging to you,

forever enticing my heart
to regain what I set adrift
by habitual disregard
and intentional wrongdoing,

forever enticing my heart
with distinct reminders
of your enduring love
and a perpetual welcome,

forever enticing my heart
with the light of your guidance,
and the texture of your touch
in the people I dearly love,

forever enticing my heart
in the quiet chambers of self,
and the determined way
you weave through everything.

~ Joyce Rupp

March

The liturgical season of Lent predominates during these four weeks. With the focus on spiritual growth, we give ourselves to the process of becoming our best and truest selves. This transformation evolves slowly but surely. When we accept the cost of polishing the mirror of our spiritual selves, we reflect ever more clearly the virtues residing within the Holy One.

Burdens

Burdens
press down with boulder heaviness,
squeeze out relief from the spent body,
foster resentment and discontent
and scrape away hope from the heart.

Burdens
erase memories of inner resilience,
tread upon the anxious mind,
stomp heavily until only a thin veneer
of self-confidence remains.

What to do, what to do.

Continue on.
Take hold of another's hand,
one that may have held yours in the past.
Hold it tightly, feel the strength
flow from that strong hand into yours.
Let it course through the exhausted maze
of your tattered self.

Let this gesture of love support you
until the day when marauders
of joy finally leave you alone,
until what has bent and burdened you
lifts the heavy weight of its visitation.

~ Joyce Rupp

Accept the Cost

I choose to live for and with those who find themselves seeing life as a long and desolate corridor with no exit signs. This is the way I'm going. If it means suffering a little bit, I'm going that way. If it means sacrificing, I'm going that way. If it means dying for them, I'm going that way. Because I heard the voice saying: do something for others.

~ Martin Luther King Jr.

Last summer a comment from an avid swimmer reawakened a valuable truth. When I mentioned seeing a crusty scab on her arm, Kathi nonchalantly explained, "I get scrapes every summer from the sharp-edged barnacles on the rocks. When my grandson started swimming with me, I told him he was bound to get some of these cuts. One day he called across the water in a proud voice: 'I got one, Grandma!' He obviously accepted the painful abrasion as the cost for a free-spirited frolic in the ocean." Kathi's comment reminded me that few of us find something rewarding without having to accept the effort, hardship, and steady determination that often accompanies what we desire.

Marilyn Melville points to something similar in her memoir *Longing, Belonging* where she tells of the immense work involved when moving into a house needing lots of fixing up. Both she and her husband spent strenuous energy "repairing endless cracks, taking down the closet and the smelly back porch, removing the broken concrete steps out back, installing a deck and new patio doors, replacing the wainscoting in the bathroom where sealing the holes provided too onerous, painting the walls four times because they were so dry, inventing ways to keep out an endless parade of mice, and pulling weeds in the backyard for four consecutive weeks." Besides this painstaking labor, their marriage suffered as the two of them "struggled and argued." Finally, after all the hard work was done, Melville recognized its worth: "I was walking through the rooms with all the beautifully painted walls, the detailed carpentry work done by my dear husband, the sun shining through the windows, and I thought to myself, *I love this place.*

As much as we want things to change, or long for what we do not yet have, some sort of mental, physical, emotional, or spiritual labor will most always be involved. Today's culture suggests that if we have enough money, the right social connections, sufficient information, the appropriate or best this or that, then exertion and discipline will not be necessary for what we want to enjoy. However, good things rarely develop all by themselves. A cost usually hides beneath what we seek.

It is natural to want the gifts of life without having to pay the price for them. I certainly find this desire in myself. There are days when I wish I could have a deeper bond with the Holy One without getting up early for meditation. I whine about the time it takes to prepare talks or pack my suitcase for air travel. At the same time, I relish arriving and being with kindred spirits, discovering fresh landscapes, and teaching on topics related to spirituality.

I spend long hours occupied in writing, often missing attendance at social events and other appealing opportunities. But when the words I've painstakingly gathered reach the publication stage, I experience a marvelous satisfaction due to the completion of my work. The same is true with family and friends. The cost of keeping these cherished relationships alive involves a commitment of deliberate, personal presence.

Likewise, the justice with which I want my country to act has to include my readiness to invest in the process. One year I joined the march of the National Women's Movement, which aimed "to harness the political power of women to create transformative social change." Before the event I heard remarks indicating how little some of the participants wanted to give of themselves for the social change they envisioned: "I'm not going. I don't like to walk in the rain. The parking area is too far away. It's going to be crowded." In the days following the march, I heard more of this reluctance to be inconvenienced or uncomfortable: "We stood for hours and couldn't march. The speeches were too long. We were told there'd be food and there wasn't any. We had to sit on the bus forever. There was no drinking water anywhere."

Those comments turned my attention to a resource about the difficult and resolute actions by those engaged in the civil rights movement. In *Across That Bridge*, Georgia congressman John Lewis describes what he and others experienced in their nonviolent and persistent efforts for racial equity. They were spit upon, verbally and physically humiliated, viciously beaten, and jailed as criminals; some ended up paying with their lives when they were brutally killed.

National Geographic journalist Victoria Pope interviewed protesters against dangerous regimes. She realized the activists could be arrested and imprisoned for speaking out, so she would ask them if she could use their names in her reporting. Pope marveled, "Usually the answer would be yes, despite the danger. I was told more than once: I want my children to know what I stood for." What courage and a price for these persons to pay for their investment in creating a more just society. Their decision to accept the cost of speaking out leads me to ask myself, "Am I willing to pay the price for the transformation I seek in my personal life and in the society to which I belong?"

Jesus accepted the cost for promoting a world of loving-kindness. His death resulted from his teachings and actions that challenged religious and political establishments. He spoke of peace, not war; of forgiveness, not vengeance; of kindness, not judgment; of mercy, not condemnation; of humility, not arrogance; and of love, not fear. He urged his followers: "If any want to become my followers, let them deny themselves and take up their cross and follow me" (Mk 8:34).

Denying self. Accepting the cost. I pray to swallow my hesitations and fear, to proceed to accept the cost, and pay it when the change I seek requires this of me.

Our Best and Truest

In this world so full of Christ, so full of blessings,
so full of things for which to be grateful,
how often I focus on the evil that surrounds me
rather than the good!

~ Macrina Wiederkehr

In *The Way of Paradox,* Cyprian Smith writes, "When we talk about 'human nature' we usually mean our weakness, frailties, and inconsistencies." Smith follows that comment with what the German mystic Meister Eckhart meant when he used the term human nature: "that which we are when we are our *best and truest.*" People intent on the spiritual life might not consider this positive dimension when speaking of human nature because of the focus on humanity's sinfulness which has long been a part of Christian preaching.

I have no doubt that I am capable of sin, of "missing the mark" as some theologians define it, but I grow tired of being told I am a sinner. All I have to do is review my day to see how I often fail to be my *best and truest.* As I grow older, I approach Lent as a time of doing something positive to reveal more of the good within me that waits to come forth instead of lamenting my wrongdoings.

What a marvelous gift it would be if, instead of being told to "remember our sins" at the opening of a eucharistic liturgy, we were first invited to pause and remember our basic worthiness. Tell a person repeatedly that she is not worthy, and the message eventually takes over her reality. She will deny, forget, or submerge her fundamental goodness and center on her "badness." I would like to go forth from a worship service inspired by the message that the best of my self longs to spill over into everything I do.

This notion comes through powerfully through the questions asked by the unknown author of *The Cloud of Unknowing* when reflecting on the woman who washed Jesus' feet with her tears and dried them with her hair:

> What did she do? Did she move down from the heights of her great desire and wallow in the memory of her failures? Did she search under every stone in the foul-smelling bog and dunghill of her life history? Did she dredge up her sins, one by one, sorrowing and weeping over each? No. Absolutely not. Why? Because God helped her to understand, by the grace in her soul, that this would not help anything.
>
> She did the very opposite. She hung up her love and her longing desire in this cloud of unknowing and attempted to learn to love something she might never clearly perceive in this life, neither by an intellectual insight nor by a true feeling of sweet, affectionate love. As a result, she paid little attention to whether or not she had been a sinner.

A turning point in my approach to sin occurred when I became acquainted with the revelations of the English anchoress, Julian of Norwich. In her visions, Julian came to view sin in relation to God's love for us, comparing our failings to a mother who allows the child to fall "so it may learn by its mistakes." Julian explains further, "When we fall [God] holds us lovingly, and graciously and swiftly raises us."

When Pope Francis reflected on saints, he noted that "[They] are not perfect models, but people *through whom God has passed*. We can compare them to the Church windows which allow light to enter in different shades of color." This metaphor speaks to me because these windows God passes through might have smudges and cracks due to stormy weather, yet the light still shines through them. So, too, with the beautiful windows of our inner selves.

In Isaiah 58:6–8 God designates what is most vital in our living: "Is not this the fast that I choose: to loose the bonds of injustice, to undo the thongs of the yoke, to let the oppressed go free, and to break every yoke? Is it not to share your bread with the hungry, and bring the homeless poor into your house; when you see the naked, to cover them, and not to hide yourself from your own kin? Then your light shall break forth like the dawn." And what is this light spreading like the brilliant glow on an eastern horizon? It is our fundamental holiness awaiting maturation in us, the same light Jesus urged his followers to shine forth.

An article in *Sojourners* magazine about the Guatemalan poet and peace advocate Julia Esquivel awakened a desire to live as my *best and truest*. Her story resurrected the part of myself that holds the potential to be unselfish, to do more to change conditions for those living on society's margins. Esquivel relinquished much of her personal comfort in an attempt to change the situation of people living in desperate poverty and a constant fear of a regime that promoted ruthless killings. Because of this Esquivel received death threats and eventually had to flee into exile, but she always lived simply and kept her heart close to those in destitution. As I read about Esquivel's life, I sighed, "My life seems a small pebble next to hers." My love immediately wanted to grow larger. Then I made a resolution to be less self-oriented and to do what I can to ease the distress of people kept on the edges of society.

Two days later I went for a walk and noticed a car nearby filled to the brim with lumps of personal belongings. *They're living in their car*, I thought and went over to speak to the depressed-looking, disheveled couple sitting inside. There it was, already on the doorstep of my heart: an opportunity be self-giving, an invitation to activate another part of my *best and truest*.

Open the Door a Crack

It can hurt to go through life with your heart open
but not as much as it does to go through life
with your heart closed.

~ James Doty

Each month when I meet with our local Circle of Compassion we spend time in small groups sharing how we have or have not experienced compassion since we last met. This past month I spoke about my struggle to work with an event coordinator at a location where I was scheduled to speak. I described my grousing to a friend about this difficulty and how my attitude toward that person changed when my friend remarked, "Oh, he must be very worried about how that will turn out." Julie, a member of our circle, turned to me and commented, "How fortunate you are for that friend to have opened the door a crack."

I marvel at how a few words can make such a difference. Julie's metaphor enabled me to grasp how my heart really *had* opened after initially closing the door by rejecting the coordinator. A crack in a doorway seems unimportant, but oh, how much light that small space can permit to enter. The crack opens up the possibility of seeing what is going on beyond the door. My friend's comment enabled me to gain a wider outlook, to move beyond irritability and judgment. Just a bit of light served to unlatch a smugly held perception in my mind about the coordinator, to see a vantage point that lay outside of my limited one. The information field expanded. Inner vision became less constricted. Light flowed in to allow me to see something missed due to my feeling pressed and unaware of what the other person might be experiencing.

The lives of individuals hold much more than my limited observation. If I forget this fact, my stresses and the problems related to people I deem difficult can look larger than they actually are. Becoming aware of the concerns of another person puts my own situation in perspective. Not that I minimize or deny the issues close at hand; rather, the expansion of my view eases the intensity of what pushes me around. This bigger picture unites my spirit with others'. In the situation of the event coordinator, instead of thinking he was making life difficult for me, I was able to enter *his* situation, to step into the anxiety he might have been feeling. This softened my heart and eased the annoyance I felt.

It seems that the door of my heart continually needs more cracking open. This happens in a variety of ways, such as when Maggie, a Boundless Compassion facilitator, quoted a friend who worked in a developing country with sparse water resources who said, "It's terrible how people in the US use so much water just to wash the soap suds out of their sinks." I'd been aware of the preciousness of water for quite a while, but for some reason, those words really stuck with me and have affected my dishwashing actions ever since.

Jennifer, my spiritual guide, cracked the door wide open one Lent regarding my negativity. After listening to my tirade about a president who was in office at the time, Jennifer lifted a small bronze heart from a nearby table. She placed the little heart in my hand as she asked, "Have you prayed for him?" No, I had not. (Oh, how much easier it is to complain than to pray for someone whose philosophy and actions oppose my own.) After that session with Jennifer, I opened the door wide enough to not only pray for the president but also to relax my grip on being upset with his seeming lack of concern for people living in severe poverty.

The first time someone pressed open the door for me came during my freshman year of college. I was placed in a dorm room with two other young women. With one of them I quickly found kinship and a sense of being at home. With the other I stood apart, questioning her "weirdness" and strong opinions. I complained about her on every home visit. A half year later, sitting at the family table, I mentioned how this roommate seemed to have improved.

My wise father looked at me and quipped, "Maybe she's not the one who's changed." Even though those words were spoken calmly, they enabled me to see my rigid opinions. I went back to school with a different attitude, dropped a lot of my judgments, and grew in appreciating my roommate for her uniqueness.

I continue to attempt to enter the larger world when confronted with disparities and when someone's ideas and actions clash with my own. I want to be able to see beyond the place where I live, to get a better sense of theirs. In doing so, my beliefs and values remain, but I become less self-righteous and tenacious about them. I am freer to move with more respect for each person, trusting the essence of divinity that resides within each of us, even when barriers between us seem ironclad.

Knowing that a wider lens allows me to step outside my own small space, I ask myself, "Can I let go of a defensive posture long enough to seek an understanding of another human being's stance? Will I do as the sign in front of a local church suggests: 'Just love everyone. I'll sort 'em out later. ~ God'?"

Ah, yes, to leave the "sorting out" to God. That will definitely take a continual cracking open of the inner door.

The Mirror Becomes Clearer

As you live deeper in the heart,
the mirror gets clearer and cleaner.

~ Jalāl ad-Dīn Rūmī

Thomas Merton, monk and mystic, taught that "we are always becoming who we already are." Fresh from the womb, we came with a magnificent freedom, totally unencumbered from cultural clutter, free from the messages telling us, "You ought to be this way. Act and think like us or we'll consider you strange and unacceptable." What a wonder we were in our infancy, peeking out at the world with indiscriminate awe, a mirror reflecting our clearest self. Then we "grew up." We gradually became unaware of how culture shapes us, how our essential goodness gets lost in the clogged, biased thought of societal norms and requirements, with adult peer pressure constantly pressing us to be other than who we truly are.

A passage in Paulo Coelho's novel *The Spy* describes how a person's interior mirror becomes badly clouded and marred with stains. At her trial, the prosecutor accuses the main character, Mata Hari, of being a despicable person. He does so with a deprecating statement: "You were beautiful, known worldwide, always envied—though never respected—in the concert halls where you appeared. Liars, what little I know of them, are people who seek popularity and recognition. Even when faced with truth, they always find a way to escape, coldly repeating what had just been said or blaming the accuser of speaking untruths. I understand that you wanted to create fantastical stories about yourself, either out of insecurity or your most visible desire to be loved at any cost."

Staying absorbed in life's exterior zone, we can easily lose touch with who we actually are. Rediscovering inner freedom means liberating our integrity until what we say and do matches the inside of our selves, like a mirror reflecting the image before it. As either the Sufi poet Jalāl ad-Dīn Rūmī or the Islamic scholar al-Ghazali wrote, "Your heart, my friend, must look like a polished mirror. You must wipe it clean of the veil of dust and particles of impurities, because your heart is destined to reflect the Light of Divine Secrets."

Ram Dass based his book *Polishing the Mirror* on that statement when he wrote about "how to live from your spiritual heart." Dass explained, "As you are pulled inward, you begin to leave behind the kinds of clinging and attachment that keep distorting and narrowing your vision. If we reflect on the qualities of Christ's love, or of equanimity, kindness or compassion, we begin to take on those qualities." The key, of course, is to be pulled inward and to allow ourselves to go there.

A question came to me from a reader: "What does it mean *to live deeper in the heart?*" I appreciated that question because it caused me to consider what "going deeper" means for myself: making the effort to be still enough to become aware of the thoughts and feelings that stir beneath life's activity as well as seeing how those thoughts and feelings affect who I say I am and want to be; noticing how my external life is or is not connected to my spiritual beliefs and values.

Going deeper includes the search for core virtuousness, which is a reflection of the loving qualities contained in the divine mirror. Just the other day the mirror of myself became a little clearer when I meditated on the good Samaritan story in Luke's gospel (10:25–37). While I've pondered that story countless times, on this particular day a brand-new insight arrived that revealed another smudge on my mirror. I noticed that the first two persons who came upon the man beaten by robbers deliberately "passed by on the other side." But the Samaritan traveler "came near to him." As soon as the words "came near to him" flew into my mental sight, I felt moved to reflect on my life. I thought about the unloving habit (the blotch on my mirror) that I had gotten into—avoiding those I do not want to be around, particularly people who do not appeal to me.

I then noticed everything the Samaritan did for the wounded individual. He disinfected the man's wound and bandaged it, "then put him on his own animal," and took him to an inn where he could rest and heal. Before the Samaritan left, he made sure there was enough money to pay for the wounded man's care. "All this," I concluded, "was for a stranger, and I cannot even sit at the same table and have more than a short conversation with someone I know but would rather avoid." In that brief meditation, I could see into my heart and knew what had to be wiped away.

Being with persons whose interior mirror is well-polished inspires me to want to attend to my own. I stopped to visit a woman in her late nineties whose mind and memory works as well as my younger one. She recently received a diagnosis of a blood condition that holds a death knell. Some of her first words let me know she had certainly polished her mirror: "All I need now is to be filled with the Holy Spirit." No fanfare. No pity party. No turn toward further medical treatments to desperately cling to physical life. I sensed a liberated heart, a surrendered soul. I marveled at this free being, about to take flight, ready to go at a moment's notice, to spread her wings fully as she prepared to depart this sphere of existence.

Her clear-heartedness inspired me to proceed into Lent with a desire to polish the mirror of my heart, to continue becoming the person I already am beneath what blurs and hides my true Self.

Slow Growth

There are things that refuse to be violated by speed, that demand at least their proper time of growth; you can't, for example, cut out the time you will leave an apple pie in the oven. If you do, you won't have an apple pie.

~ Caryll Houselander

Lent begins with Ash Wednesday's challenging word: "Repent." This six-letter word with its gigantic exhortation takes us into six weeks of resolve to improve our spiritual life. As we evaluate what needs tending, it's not unusual to feel our hope for transformation swallowed by the discouraging thought that we're not all that different now than we were on the previous Lent. Maybe we even succumb to the woeful judgement that the hoped-for growth will never happen.

When I look at what requires transformation in my life, I notice how certain patterns continue to cultivate unwanted behavior. My good intentions slide away. I fail to grow beyond barriers my ego chooses to erect. When these thoughts start yanking me toward the doldrums of hopelessness, it's time to pause and take an honest look at the areas of my life that *have* ripened with gospel teachings. Without a backward glance at where I have changed for the better, I lose confidence in the possibility of future progress.

Last summer an experience awakened me to the value of peering into my history in order to accept the truth of my spiritual growth. While attending a conference at my religious community's motherhouse, I went for a daily walk. On the third morning, a tall, wide-branched, fully-leafed linden tree practically reached out and put a stop sign in front of me. The breadth, depth, and height of the intensely green tree drew me into its beauty and extended an invitation to stand beneath the dense foliage.

My heart leapt with amazement as I looked up into the wide sweep of thickly-leafed branches hiding my view of the canopy. If a tree could smile, the linden was doing that. I stood in awed attention, listening to the tree's silent voice: "Do you remember when you first knew me? You had an office over there, by that window on the lower level. That's where you sat by the old wooden desk, intent on writing your first book thirty-some years ago. How uncertain and unsteady you were. I tried to give you courage and hope when you and I met every day during that tentative year."

I continued to gaze into the fullness of the linden, marveling at its stature, the immense growth from the thin sapling I first knew to the now expansive loveliness. Then the tree revealed another feature—an image of my spiritual growth. As I looked backward through those years, I felt astonished by the major changes within myself, the evolving, personal transformation. I never dreamt my inner life would alter as much as it had when the young tree was not much taller than myself. So now, when my days are overly full and I start questioning if I'll ever leave my old, useless habits behind or long for spiritual transformation to come much more quickly than it does, I remember that moment when the linden tree reached out and spoke to me.

That morning visit with its unexpected view of my spiritual history led me to think about each person having his or her own tree. Oh, maybe not a real tree, but some piece of life from the past that provides a valuable perspective from that point until the present. This long view discloses the growth-filled aspects that have come forth from oneself, that have become more settled and yield greater harmony with God and others. There's always more maturation to follow, but failing to admit inner progress is failing to acknowledge the presence and effect of divine grace.

No one "has it completely together." Every one of us has more growing to do. Robert Wicks recognizes this in *Night Call*, "It is not the amount of darkness in the world or in one's self that matters. . . . It is how one stands in that darkness that makes the essential difference." And how *do* we stand? With confidence and patience, trusting in our intentions and efforts, and counting on divine grace to transform what still awaits maturation.

Several evaluations from a recent retreat on compassion brought me back to that graced insight of last summer. One person assessed the retreat with "I think I flunked compassion; I thought I'd leave with having a better relationship with my daughter." Another re- treatant wrote, "I hoped I'd be able to feel better about elected of- ficials." These comments reminded me that people today expect speedy transformation. Because we can communicate with others instantaneously and locate information with a few touches on an electronic device, our impatience with personal growth seems like a natural consequence.

Growth takes place while on the journey, not at the goal post. Think of the gestation process. Humans normally linger for nine months in their mothers' wombs. Elephants wait almost two years before being birthed. And if you were a saguaro cactus in an Arizo- na desert, you'd only grow an infinitesimal bit in a year, becoming taller by one and a half inches in the first eight years. Yes, that's right, one and a half inches in eight years. Nothing in a vegetable garden springs up instantly (except the weeds). Every growing thing entails a certain passage of time to mature into its fullness.

In her essay "About Practice, Clear Seeing, and Keeping the Faith," Sylvia Boorstein emphasizes the slow process of spiritual growth by describing a cartoon: "The father of a desert clan travel- ing astride their camels is chiding his children (riding behind him on baby camels) saying, 'Stop asking "Are we there yet?" We're *nomads* for crying out loud.'" Boorstein adds, "More and more these days I hear myself talking about faith in (and for) the journey rather than the imagined destination."

If we were making a thousand-mile trip, we would not give up midway and turn back, saying "This is just too long." No, we would go mile by mile and eventually come to where we hoped to arrive. So, too, with our spiritual growth. Slowly but surely, we grow and change. Slowly, we arrive.

Hold My Hand

Companion of hurting hearts,
When peace of mind and gentleness of heart slip away,
hold my hand.
When I lose sight of my worthiness and self-esteem,
hold my hand.
When unrealistic expectations crowd out joy and satisfaction,
hold my hand.
When I forget to breathe in and listen to my inner being,
hold my hand.
When fear of vulnerability keeps me from seeking assistance,
hold my hand.
When I stumble and fall on the path of doing too much,
hold my hand.
When something I have believed in disintegrates into ashes,
hold my hand.
When the distress of others overwhelms my compassion,
hold my hand.
When I cannot find comfort in Earth's natural beauty,
hold my hand.
When love suffers from the lost desire to be invested and faithful,
hold my hand.
When the road of life before me appears useless and deserted,
hold my hand.
When a sense of your presence flees from my awareness,
hold my hand.

Tenderhearted One, you continually walk with me. I am not alone when my spirit droops in the hazy grayness of life. Keep teaching me how necessary it is to care well for myself, to trust that the valley of darkness I walk through is a part of the process of transformation. I place my hand in yours once again, and move forward with hope in your loving presence.

~ Joyce Rupp

April

Although we cannot force joy to dance within us, it often erupts with the emergence of springtime and the glorious feast of the Resurrection. We gain renewed hope to break free from obstacles that imprison our passion for life. Happiness claps its hands and cheers us on. We rejoice in the good fortune and unfolding gladness arriving for others and ourselves.

April Arrival

Therefore my heart is glad,
and my soul rejoices.

~ Psalm 16:9

April arrives with droplets
of rain in her morning eyes;
bird chatter rinses the air
with their awakening joy.

And is my heart glad?
Does my soul rejoice?

Only for a passing interlude
when expectations fall silent
and the heavy footsteps depart
from the worn calendar.

My soul peeks into the dawn,
aware of the thin aperture
allowing for a possible release
from what muffles the gladness.

She would swing the door wide,
dance with the jubilation of angels,
if only my weary, galloping self
would sit down and shut up.

~ Joyce Rupp

Born for Joy

Write your sorrows in sand and etch your joys in stone.

~ Ancient Chinese Proverb

"Where do you find your joy?" Cindy's question surfaced in our conversation about dismal conditions here and elsewhere on the planet. I stumbled and mumbled a few words in response to Cindy's query, but I couldn't offer much that day. The next morning when I considered that question more closely, I gathered a surprisingly long list of reasons why I continue to carry a quiet joy within me. None had a megaphone quality, but each reason provided definite worth for keeping this valuable gift close by. Among the sources: a sliver of sunshine after lengthy seasonal gloominess, the surprise of a stranger's kindness, hundreds of geese circling above the lake, the taste of truth in a book, morning coffee, a belly-laugh-inducing movie, felt kinship in communal prayer, the easy rhythm of a long walk, a friend's poem, and the harmonious melody of a favorite song.

Joy often disguises itself in layers of what appears disconcerting and troublesome. This might happen because the focus of life tends toward "what is wrong" rather than "what goes well." When pleasure and satisfaction become buried in such things as the press of constant demands, home responsibilities, care of others, and tending personal illness, it is understandable that the goodness in life and the enjoyment of it soon fades away.

I know people who retain their contentment no matter how dismal and difficult their situation. Their lives hold more than average adversity, but they somehow manage to retain a foundational contentment. It's not that they deny their hardships. Rather, they do not let these misfortunes conquer their ability to appreciate the positive things that come their way. Within them a deep river of peace flows on and on; nothing stops or completely drains its movement. They have learned and accepted that joy never totally dies unless we allow this to occur.

"Those who have not found their true wealth, which is the radiant joy of Being and the deep, unshakable peace that comes with it, are beggars, even if they have great material wealth," writes Eckhart Tolle in *The Power of Now*. He then explains why he uses "beggars": "They are looking outside for scraps of pleasure or fulfillment, for validation, security, or love, while they have a treasure within that not only includes all those things but is infinitely greater than anything the world can offer."

I think part of the secret to claiming joy lies in Mary Oliver's poem "Mindful" where she tells us she was born for joy, that she looks, listens, and loses herself in what she notices around her. In one of her prose poems, "Don't Hesitate," Oliver encourages her reader to not waver in accepting joy when this gift arrives. She also wisely counsels to not fear joy's "plenty," with the reminder that "joy is not made to be a crumb."

We learn from this observant poet that joy doesn't hang around without a little effort to keep it there. People who regularly experience this gift tend to be deliberate in noticing something, however small, that prompts wonder and gratitude. This finding, of course, requires some attentiveness, as Christina Feldmann notes in *Boundless Heart:* "Joy is concerned with reclaiming that capacity within ourselves, to be able to see anew. It is so clear to us that when our eyes are tired, the world appears bleak. When our hearts are jaded and desensitized, the world becomes colorless and flat. The sensitive, mindful heart perceives value and worth in all things. . . . There is a powerful link between mindfulness and joy and the effect it has upon perception."

People knowingly or unknowingly can shred our enthusiasm. A saying I heard some time ago holds me steady in troubled times: "Don't let them steal your joy." Keeping joy alive does not mean we let go of compassion or that we stop tending to our own or others' wounds. Joy does not negate life's tough things. It maintains hope in the midst of them. Even small, steady movements of gladness are able to sustain us.

Besides being able to lessen our joy, people also have the capacity to enliven it. Yesterday I met Jack Lemmon on the bike trail. Well, it wasn't the actual actor; this man just looked a lot like him. Walking his small dachshund, "Jack" shouted out a joy-filled morning greeting while he was still fifteen yards away: "Beautiful day, isn't it?" I called back, "Yes, makes you want to bottle it up for those sweltering days ahead." When "Jack" drew near, I saw his huge smile and a glint in his eyes: a happy man and his happy dog. I felt their joy. It was so close that it crowded out the glumness that had started my day. I think that man knew how the poet Anne Sexton concluded her "Welcome Morning": "The Joy that isn't shared, I've heard, dies young."

The Easter stories in the gospels and the accompanying liturgical prayers also encourage us to regain our joy. This natural response to the depictions of Jesus' Resurrection reveals the central motive: the return of a loving presence thought to be lost. Instead of never returning, this love appears in fresh form. Those who chose to be open and aware of the risen Christ found their joy restored in ways they could not have imagined.

Joy is not something to be forced. This quality is not a fake, paste-on-a-smile sort of thing. It often shows up unexpectedly or when there is enough inner space for it to settle in us. I agree with Mary Oliver: we are born for joy. Each day now when I wake in the morning I whisper to my deeper self: "You were born for joy."

And so are you.

Breaking the Chains

Some sat in darkness and in gloom,
>prisoners in misery and in irons. . . .
They cried to the LORD in their trouble,
>and [God] saved them from their distress,
[God] brought them out of darkness and gloom,
>and broke their bonds asunder.

~ Psalm 107:10, 13–14

I spent most of a week walking for hours each day on the magnificent Oregon coast. One morning I noticed how much delight I felt. I also observed this in others: a father and daughter screamed in false fright as they held hands and leapt into the incoming waves; a blonde-haired girl in a bright blue party dress laughed at the water circling her feet; people of all sizes and ages smiled as they stooped over to pick up shells and other objects capturing their curiosity; a middle-aged woman lay flat-bellied on her surfboard and erupted with triumphant shouts as the waves lifted her to shore. Everywhere slivers of enjoyment appeared, sounding in the voices of children building sandcastles and in the joined hands of elderly companions as they strolled the sandy beach.

As I walked along, I thought, *This place draws forth joy*. It seemed to me that the rhythm of the ocean allowed each person there to temporarily leave behind the stress and strain that clog our lives and that people drag around every day. The usual tumbles and turns wrenching away the delight of life and the pressured schedules that clamp down on simple pleasures temporarily halted.

After returning home I wondered if it might be possible to retain the quiet satisfaction that readily took over my spirit at the ocean.

The answer came when I joined other women for our Tuesday morning prayer. Our facilitator that day chose a theme from *The Cup of Our Life:* "Recognizing Resistances." The chapter opens with a quote from Macrina Wiederkehr: "I am entirely ready to have the chains that keep me bound be broken. I am entirely ready for the walls I've built around myself to be torn down. I am entirely ready to give up my need to control every situation. I am entirely ready to let go of my resentments. I am entirely ready to grow up."

As I heard this, I realized, *That's it. If I could live that kind of "readiness" regarding my daily tasks and the unwanted aspects, joy would find a more lasting home inside of me.* Resisting what is, fighting off what I do not want, trying to force everything to turn out positively, forgetting how the Holy One guides and directs, throwing mental tantrums when life gets messy or painful—yes, all of this and more, are bound to keep the kind of happiness experienced on the shores of the Pacific Ocean from residing in my being.

When I face obstacles, I have a variety of options for how to respond. Some choices de-energize me and shut out joy; others re-energize and enhance joy. When I pause to listen closely, I am most often led to a freeing decision rather than to one that increases the heaviness manacling me to the concrete floor of my ego—the part of me that always wants what it wants when it wants it and throws a hissy-fit when it cannot have it.

When I face these kinds of choices, I know I need to turn to a power greater than myself for assistance to move beyond the restraints. As Psalm 107 indicates, there's a moment when I find myself crying out to the Holy One that I may have wisdom and strength to break what binds my peace and joy. When this happens, I feel like Peter imprisoned in chains, the angel coming in the dark of night, breaking those restraints and leading the disciple to freedom (see Acts 12:3–19).

Nature often teaches me about moving from obstacles to freedom from them. When I brought overseas visitors to the area of the Black Hills in South Dakota, I arose early one morning and went by myself to walk the loop around a nearby lake. It was early April, and I missed the sign about possible ice on the path. Not long after I started walking, I faced an unwelcome sight: huge boulders and the path between them filled with a grim layer of ice. I looked ahead and saw more of the same. I had no hiking boots. I knew I could fall and break a bone, which would ruin the trip for my friends. I paused. What to do? In that silence, ever so softly I sensed where I might go.

I turned around, and after a short jaunt, I found a way to walk into the woods. A path there took me on soft pine needles among evergreen trees to a place above the icy boulders where I could look out onto immense pillars of sandstone and beyond to the beautiful valley. In this place I found a small open space among the stones where I could sit, put my head back on the rocks, and rest my feet in front of me on a flat stone. I felt held by those ancient parts of earth and cradled by the One who led me beyond the blockage to that surprising embrace of pleasure.

Sometimes turning away from an obstacle is not easy to do. And sometimes it will not bring immediate relief as the new path did for me. But if we turn inward when something or someone blocks the way ahead, when we pray through a difficult situation, eventually we turn the corner and discover a peace-filled place within ourselves.

The flow of life will not always be upbeat. There will be periods when pain of body, mind, or spirit temporarily thrusts joy aside. This is to be expected. I will not always feel content, but inner peace can remain constant. That is, if my resistances cease and I am ready to have the chains broken.

Being Happy for Others

We find gladness in the midst of the gladness
of another, joy in the happiness of another,
appreciation for the many ways our lives
and our hearts are touched by the life
and heart of another.

~ Christina Feldman

Can we be happy for those who enjoy what we desire and do not have? This question arose in me while reflecting on the Easter stories. I noticed how few disciples of Jesus actually received the gift of a direct encounter with his risen presence. Some caught a few glimpses of him, but many did not even have that. Did those who toiled and dedicated themselves to learn and share his teachings feel disappointed for not having this direct experience? Did they covet that encounter? Luke's gospel describes two disciples who were "looking sad" as they plodded back to their hometown. When asked about their gloominess, they mumbled downheartedly about reports of others who visited the tomb and saw a vision of angels, insisting he was alive. But these two had no such personal contact and were giving up hope of this ever happening (see Lk 24:13–35).

Their emotional response is no stranger to my heart. During a bitterly cold winter a begrudging voice in me tried to take over my usually positive outlook. This chiding voice daily reminded me of friends and colleagues who were finding refuge from the seasonal bleakness by traveling to warmer locations. It seemed as though every week someone else slipped away for a delicious break while I worked doggedly with no hope for a leisurely respite.

This "poor me" whining finally hushed when a memory surfaced of an incident three years earlier. In preparation for going to Iona, Scotland, for a retreat on that mystical island, I went to a discount store to buy a pair of boots. When I mentioned where I was going to the clerk who waited on me, she expressed enthusiasm about my anticipated trip. As I left the store with my new boots it occurred to me that she most probably could not afford to go anywhere outside the country, maybe not even have any type of vacation. Yet there she was, genuinely happy for me.

The memory of that incident humbled me and led to my sincerely rejoicing with those I had envied. "This parallels unconditional love," I decided, "a movement of the heart untainted by self-interest. I can be happy for others whose advantage is not mine." Buddhism refers to this generous joy as *mudita*. This term implies being happy for another's prosperity and is sometimes referred to as "sympathetic joy" or "empathic joy." With *mudita*, we allow ourselves to feel happy for someone else without a begrudging self-pity.

Mudita arises within a generous heart free from resentment and ill will. In *The Magnanimous Heart*, Narayan Helen Liebenson comments, "It seems especially difficult to experience empathic joy, joy for the good fortune of others. The reason may be that in the competitive culture we live in, comparing ourselves to others appears to be necessary, especially given the lack of a safety net for so many. . . . We imagine that if someone else is joyful we will not be."

Envy casts desirous eyes toward what other people have: superior health, an easier life, a successful marriage, an attractive body, a bigger home, greater intelligence, financial ease, a newer car, long-lasting friendships, enhanced social skills, "perfect" children, and other perceived assets. Envy generates the jealous thought: *They have it. I don't have it. I wish I did. I think I should.* The envious heart sulks, thinks negatively, and sometimes even goes so far as to wish harm to another, hoping they will lose what they have.

There will always be someone who has more of something than we do. Can we rejoice with those whose spiritual lives seem to flow smoothly when ours feel stuck in the mud? Can we affirm another's talents that are not ours? Can we support wholeheartedly those whose childhood did not contain the pain that ours did? Can we reach out with compassion to the person whose illness is the exception while our chronic poor health rarely subsides? Can we be glad for other people's success or material wealth?

When a fixated longing takes over, recognition of our own prosperity slides away. Envy smothers gratitude. Desire for what is lacking muscles its way in, leading to dissatisfaction. It burglarizes joy. Envy diverts attention from the good that already exists. In my own situation, I neglected to see how much I enjoyed the evenings of darkness that allowed for extended, satisfying gatherings of friends, refreshing walks in fresh snowfalls and brilliant starry skies, plus the extra time for reading books that piled high during summer's feverish activity. I also abandoned my awareness of winter's gift of solitude and the nurturing space it provided for writing. Gratitude momentarily went down the drain when I let my grumpy envy pull me away from recognizing those pleasurable gifts.

I have also gained encouragement from generous-hearted persons who are happy for others even though their life lacks comparable satisfactions. I've witnessed people with financial insecurity extend a gracious welcome to affluent relatives, individuals with recurring clinical depression express gladness for the good health of others, widows and widowers celebrate others' love by participating in gatherings with those who have spousal companionship, childless women rejoice at the birth of a friend's newborn, and workers cheer on their retired colleagues in spite of their own need to work long past retirement age.

In *Boundless Heart*, when Christina Feldman explores what brings joy, she identifies *mudita* as a central source: "This is a significant aspect of the fabric of joy, tempering our tendencies to envy others in ways that we feel ourselves to be deprived or inadequate, and to come to know a selfless joy in the face of another's happiness." *A selfless joy.* That sums up the priceless decision to share in another's good fortune without trying to claim it for our own possession.

Trying to Make It Happen

When we have an attachment to results,
we tend to have a hard time giving up control.
When we stop trying to control events,
they fall into a natural order, an order that works.

~ Marianne Williamson

Have you ever planned for an adventure, pictured it with anticipation, and worked out all the details with confidence it would turn out just like you envisioned? One of the times I fell into this deception of thinking I could control events came about while spending a week of solitude with a writing friend at a hunter's lodge in eastern Oklahoma. The attractive lodge stands nobly on a craggy bluff overlooking the wide Arkansas River. Writing glides along comfortably in this place due to the exquisite silence and natural beauty suffusing the many acres of woodland, hidden ponds, and broad meadows.

I am definitely not a hunter, but I longed to see some of the wild creatures inhabiting the area, so I decided to spend a night in one of the hunting blinds. As I planned for this adventure, I conjured up all sorts of marvelous "God-moments" that would occur: the sight of shy bobcats and herds of deer, a glimpse of newborn coyote pups I'd heard yipping in the night, waterfowl on the pond, and of course, an exquisite sunrise.

When I viewed the blind from the outside earlier in the day, it looked quite adequate for my plan. The square, enclosed wooden structure stood about fifteen feet off the ground with two small, oblong windows near the top of one side. The ladder to the blind and the space itself appeared sturdy and safe. As I surveyed the situation, I thought, *Perfect. I'm going to really feel the Holy One's presence here.*

The night air felt calm as I left the lodge to walk the mile to the hunting blind, carrying sleeping bag, pillow, binoculars, and water bottle. But no sooner had I begun to climb the ladder to the blind when an enormous wind swept into the darkness. I did not know that weather warnings of thirty-five to fifty miles per hour winds had been issued for the area. I also did not gauge the inner space well. I found that my five-foot, two-inch body barely fit, even when I lay down diagonally. To complicate matters, the metal chair in the middle of that tight space had been bolted down, so I could not move it to create a bit more room.

All night long the wind howled while I shivered in a fetal position from the unexpected freezing temperature. I could hear nothing except the moan and wild banging of the heavily limbed oak trees above me, causing me concern at their possibly breaking off and crushing both the hunting blind and me. At 5 a.m., I was wide awake with relief that morning had arrived. But then some euphoric energy arose with the thought, *Oh, good, now the animals will appear.* I watched and waited for two hours in the disappointing, clouded dawn, but all I saw was a fat skunk ambling by.

I learned a valuable lesson that night: I cannot determine and control when and how a "God-moment" arrives. I wanted to *make it happen,* but nothing turned out as I expected; no ecstatic response to nature, no comforting sense of divine presence, no awesome sounds or views of anything I hoped to experience. I was humbly forced to admit that spiritual events are not in my power to create and control. Nor do they turn out the way I envision.

But that night *did* contain some spiritual moments. Being in the hunter's blind during that fearsome wind led me to surrender myself into the Creator's care when terror about being injured or killed grabbed hold of me. My prayer grew in strength that challenging night, and I gained more empathy as I lay there in the cramped space, thinking of what a prisoner in solitary confinement, an immigrant squeezed between others in the back of a truck, or a homeless person sleeping out in the cold might go through.

As Easter approaches, I recognize the tendency to program oneself into having an emotional high. It's not uncommon to have an expectation of feeling elated. The gospel accounts of the disciples' joyous recognition of the risen Christ indirectly set us up for this. Yet, we may feel anything but joyous. We might be weighed down with sadness or have unresolved problems embedded in our spirits. No matter how hard we try to force this dismay to depart, these inner disturbances stick firmly with us.

In *Fresh Bread*, I described how "little Easters await us when we're having a difficult time summoning a big amount of gladness. These moments consist of comments or actions we tend to overlook in our hope of having a glorious emotional response." I recall the day my spirit moved from a troubling agitation to an awakened awareness. My friend Lisa and I stood chatting after the Easter Vigil, reflecting on the mysteries contained in the Resurrection narratives. Lisa commented, "Maybe the stories aren't so much about women being chosen to announce the Resurrection as it was a natural consequence of their lives. Women were the ones who spent time with the dead. Women entered the smelly, dark tomb prepared to anoint cold flesh. That was how they discovered the body of Jesus was not there and how their joy eventually surfaced."

I could sense a slight turning within me as Lisa spoke. A little Easter started to move in. The thought of dedicated women deliberately going toward what would be unpleasant and doing this out of loving dedication—that suggestion stirred my desire to do a similar sort of thing—to go toward what I wanted to avoid, particularly in a current, struggling relationship.

I didn't feel elation as I drove home, but I did feel somewhat hopeful in relearning that "Alleluia feelings" cannot be forced at Easter any more than I could conjure up a spiritual experience in the hunter's blind. And yet, little stirrings do occur. If the mind and heart are open, we may be visited by them, those seemingly insignificant and unexpected occurrences that expand faith and increase hope. But these moments are not ours to create or control.

We trust. We wait. We stay open. We avoid pushing. Eventually, the risen One visits us in a surprising and unexpected way.

Genuine Happiness

You don't do happiness.
You receive it.

~ **Natalie Goldberg**

When author Natalie Goldberg was in bed with a nasty flu, she felt physically miserable but also extremely happy for the opportunity to sleep and read. She reflects in "Waking Up to Happiness," that she was equally aware "that as soon as my energy returned I'd plunge back into mad activity, full of passion. I was lucky because I loved most of what I did in life, but as I lay in bed I realized passion is different than happiness. You don't *do* happiness. You receive it. It's like a water table under the earth. It's available to everyone but we can only tap it, have it run up through us, when we're still. A well that darts around can never draw water."

Goldberg adds, "We misinterpret success, desire, enterprise, and the things we love as the state of happiness. Usually, we don't consider happiness because we're too busy dashing after life, defending, building, developing, even fighting, asserting, arguing. We're in the scramble—lively, engaged. So where does happiness come in? It's a give and take, a meeting of inside and outside. . . . Happiness is shy. It wants you to know it. You can't be greedy. You can't be numb—or ignorant. The bashful girl of happiness needs your kind attention. Then she'll come forward. And you won't have to be sick to find her."

"Am I happy?" Twenty years ago, I continually asked myself that question because I did not always have positive, uplifting feelings. I was unable to get life to go the way I insisted, couldn't keep people I loved from illness and death, and never found enough time for what

I wanted to be and do. But as the years passed, I realized that happiness isn't about having life neatly ordered or feeling exuberant. I've come to understand that happiness flows from peace of mind and heart no matter what happens. Life is not always going to unfold according to my preferences. People may not respond in the way I wish. Inner and outer storms will come and go. Joy will infuse my life and then abate. Such is the human journey. If I can receive what is, seeing each piece of life as a part of a whole needed for growth, then I am content. Then I am happy.

Two experiences catapulted me into a fuller understanding of happiness. I viewed a thought-provoking documentary titled *Happy*. In the film, a group of leading social scientists discover in their research that being happy is what most human beings desire more than anything else. They also learn that if the basic needs of life are met, happiness can follow.

The film's setting opens with a slum in Kolkata, India. A man washes his feet with a bucket of water, then turns to wave goodbye to his children who play in the dirt. The slender man assures the interviewer that he is happy with his life. He points to his home, a partially boarded shack with holes in the roof that let in rain during the monsoon season. Still, he smiles a lot and insists he is happy because his family has enough food to eat, and he has work as a rickshaw driver. As they interview other "happy people," the scientists agree that the accumulation of wealth is not what leads to happiness.

The second experience occurred a day after viewing that film. While traveling on the freeway, my car had a flat tire. I pulled off the road as far as possible, but my small vehicle still shook fiercely every time a large truck passed. I called for roadside assistance and was informed it would be at least an hour before someone arrived. I decided to accept the situation by patiently waiting in my car and taking the time for reflection. I had barely made that decision when a knock at the window startled me. There stood a middle aged, bald-headed man in a business suit. He introduced himself as Herb and smiled as he explained, "I passed by but something in me said I had to turn around and come back to help you." I hesitated, thinking of the time and effort for him to change the tire. I almost declined with "Thanks, assistance is coming," but a certain eagerness in his voice stopped me.

As Herb replaced the tire, he told me about his having a stroke and then, more recently, coping with cancer. He rubbed his bald head and added, "That's what led to this." After replacing the tire, he wobbled up from his kneeling posture and told me about the volunteer work he now does with children who have cancer. Just that morning he received word about the death of a six-year-old especially dear to him. Tears came to Herb's eyes as he explained, "That's why I stopped. I knew I had to do something to honor that young boy's life. I had to help you. I'm so glad I could do this."

While we stood there with the strong wind and heavy traffic whipping past us, I knew I was in the presence of a kind-hearted man who had circled death's rim. He knew about "happy" in a way I had not known. Life was not about how much success or money Herb accumulated. Life was about appreciation for life itself, being ⚓ on the lookout for unexpected situations to offer assistance, and trying to relieve distress with gestures of goodwill that brought joy.

Herb is the epitome of what Archbishop Desmond Tutu describes in *The Book of Joy:* "In order to be a happy person, we need to live from the compassionate part of our nature and to have a sense of responsibility toward others and the world we live in."

Hearken, Hope, Hearken

Source of Hope,
your unexpected appearances
to the brokenhearted disciples
assured them of your unconquerable love.

Draw us close to you when we travel
our Emmaus roads of vanished hope.
Veer us away from wounding negativity
and shriveled enthusiasm.

Navigate and encourage us
to go beyond tidal waves of inner strife,
and scary apprehensions filled
with doomsday predictions and fears.

Bring us to a glad remembrance
of your empty tomb and risen life
when we feel like giving up
on the possibility of future change.

Let us look with fresh eyes of the heart
and remember your companionship;
we can draw strength from your presence
when the winding currents of adversity
threaten to steal the last piece of serenity.

Breathe hope in us.
Again and again.
We dare not let this virtue die.

~ Joyce Rupp

May

The vibrant movement of the divine Spirit in us flows unceasingly. This dynamic energy guides our inner direction. We learn anew to listen closely for the echo of this stirring presence. With the Spirit's potent encouragement, we boot out old fears, regain our balance, embrace our empowerment, and rejoice in the restored peace filling our being.

A Wing and a Hand

A movement like the soft wing
of an angel or a gentle hand,
leading my awareness toward
what will bend a wayward focus
and welcome a wandering heart,
guidance for undivided purpose,
courage for the ongoing journey.

Gratitude for this regal gift
of a Someone, a silent presence
much larger, deeper, stronger
than I could begin to envision,
a love completely given without
my asking, without knowing
how much I need what is offered.

This Earthling I am, breathing
in the pale shallows of only
one realm, one conscious space,
yet occasionally drawn toward
a wildly free Spirit traversing easily
the unbounded spheres of love.

Today this bounded Earthling senses
there is more, so much more;
believes because of a kindly touch,
the movement of a wing and a guiding
hand leading toward the Light.

~ Joyce Rupp

The Wild Flow of Energy

It is impossible to stop the well of energy and the well of light and the well of life that is inside of you. You might calm it and quell it, but it will still rise up within you.

~John O'Donohue

If you are confined to using a wheelchair, dealing with a challenging illness, struggling to make it through the bleakness of a lost relationship, a tough job, or long-lasting grief, you might think to yourself, *Yeah, right, "the wild flow of energy"—it certainly isn't there for me.* But it is. Not in the way you presume this energy to be, but in a way that touches your deeper self.

In *Walking in Wonder,* when Celtic poet John O'Donohue refers to the "wild flow of energy," he uses a twofold definition of wild: something natural or growing untamed in its own habitat and also a dynamic movement. Long ago in a physics class I learned about two basic forms of energy: active and potential. The internet describes energy as "an ability" to do something. It is "how things change and move." Even though we probably pay little attention, we have active energy working steadily in our body. Every breath and every heartbeat involve an unseen movement to sustain our physical life.

Along with active energy, a potential energy also rests in us. Anthony deMello, S.J., tells the story of some five-thousand-year-old grains of wheat found in an Egyptian tomb. To everyone's amazement, when someone planted those seeds, the grains sprouted. He stresses how the "life and energy" remained in those seeds through the centuries. It just took someone to plant them so their dormant life could spring into action. He then compares this to our spiritual life, how the potential in the seeds of our spiritual growth need to be "sown in a receptive, fertile heart." We have potential characteristics and virtues yet to awaken and be nursed into action.

The liturgical feasts of Easter and Pentecost involve an inherent, transformative energy, both active and potential, a movement of graced vitality with the power to further our spiritual transformation. Notice the way scripture speaks about the energy of the Resurrection. When the body of Jesus lay in the tomb, the latent life within him waited to be activated. Only when Jesus *"was raised* from the dead" did this dormant energy surge through his physical form. The Holy One entered the stillness of his inertia and danced fresh vitality through him. A restored energy prompted Jesus to go forth from the tomb as the resurrected Christ. Vibrancy awakened in him—a wild current of divinity—so fresh and energizing that even an intimate friend like Mary of Magdala did not recognize his vibrant form (see Gal 1:1; 1 Cor 15:4; Acts 2:32, 10:40, 13:30; Rom 6:14, 8:11).

John's Gospel presents the death of Lazarus, friend of Jesus, as a prelude to the dynamic movement from death into life. Like Jesus, Lazarus could not have his interior energy empowered by his own efforts. Only when he heard "Lazarus, come out!" did he begin to stir. Even then, the burial shrouds encasing his body had to be unwrapped by others. Lazarus could not manage the movement from potential to active energy by himself (see Jn 11:38–44).

Similar to an electrical socket lacking the ability to be a conduit of energy until a lamp is plugged into that socket to receive stored energy, so it is with our relation to divine life. We need a connection with the Holy One in order for this impending dynamism to affect us. The divine current or "touch" we receive enables our potential virtues to be sparked alive in us.

Mary Ford-Grabowski suggests in *Stations of the Light* that the tomb-time of Jesus was like that of a "dark, silent fertility" coming alive with the energy of light. In this seemingly dead space, "the tomb opens like a womb giving birth. . . . Throughout the subsequent fifty days of the first Easter season, the light grows increasingly brighter. The journey that began in the first light of dawn on Easter Sunday morning progresses through varying degrees of sunlight to its culmination in the blazing fiery light of Pentecost."

It is, of course, in that profound event of Pentecost that those present experienced the Spirit's energy: "Divided tongues, as of fire, appeared among them, and a tongue rested on each of them" (Acts 2:3). Could there be a more direct expression of the powerful energy of divinity entering the human spirit than fire, an element created when an energetic chemical reaction occurs due to the combination of oxygen and some kind of fuel? Recall the other description of Pentecost as a rushing sound of the Spirit entering the room. This divine life force comes in the form of another type of energy—"like the rush of a violent wind" (Acts 2:2). This potent, spiritual dynamism swept through the minds and hearts of those present and they were never the same.

When I experience this divine movement, it usually happens in ordinary ways, such as reading a stimulating quote that prompts me to see a deeper meaning, recognizing the love binding my heart with another's, hearing inspiring stories of people's kindheartedness, a sudden awareness that prompts me to want to bring a certain virtue into action, or feeling a quiet peacefulness when praying at dawn. Like a sleeping bird awakening and giving birth to song after its head has been tucked under her wing, I sense a stirring inside. I become alert to what seems to be emerging. A feeling of aliveness resurrects in the deadened areas of my being.

How has the Spirit's wild flow of energy visited and influenced your soul? Sit in the "upper room" of your daily life, and you will find it there.

Grace Has No Expiration Date

Grace is resilience. Grace is forgiveness.
It is healing. It is revelation, the oneness
of all being. It is enlightenment. It is faith.

~ Karen Hering

"Grief has a long shelf life. It will wait for as long as it takes to be tended." This statement by a speaker at a conference came to mind at the recent feast of Pentecost. I thought, *Grace, too, has a long shelf life and will wait to be tended. Grace has no expiration date.*

I've come to know grace not as a thing but as the loving movement of the Holy One. Grace consists of a sacred presence ready to mobilize us into action. When allowed to enter our lives, this brings motivation, courage, insight, guidance—whatever our spiritual growth requires—including indispensable fruits or gifts of the Spirit such as those enumerated in Galatians 5:22: "love, joy, peace, patience, kindness, generosity, faithfulness."

When I look into the journals I've kept through the years, I see how grace has affected my life. Moving through those pages is like sifting through the ups and downs of my spiritual journey. There I find what I have forgotten, including words spoken that comforted me in times of sorrow, events that challenged my stubborn thoughts, swift and surprising moments of nature that drew me to insight and sweet harmony with the sacred, along with countless times when something I read or heard went *zing* inside of me. I can see evidence everywhere of how the divine Spirit has swept through my life and repeatedly caught my attention.

Zen teacher Adyashanti also knows the power and benefit of grace. He writes, "Sometimes grace is soft and beautiful. It appears as insight. It comes as a sudden understanding, or maybe just the blossoming of our hearts, the breaking open of our emotional bodies so that we can feel more deeply and connect with what is and with each other in a deeper way. Grace can also be quite fierce. There are times in life that are very, very trying. At times, grace might be hard to recognize, but as we think back to these powerful times in our lives, we can start to see the great gift that was received."

And so it is that the movement of this loving Spirit can startle us by shaking loose our false moorings. I remember the phone call fifteen years ago from a man who related a frightening dream. That dream served to uproot him from years of daily drunkenness and being high on drugs to a life free from those addictive behaviors. I also recall a pastor telling me that he could hardly believe what happened in the short visit to a homebound parishioner. After months of the pastor's debilitating depression, he felt the fresh air of peace sweep through his mind and heart as he left the house.

Grace also arrives with less of a jolt and more of the steady movement of a little creek humming its way along until we finally pause to listen to the flowing stream's music and allow it to make a home in us. Being receptive to grace is as simple as turning the heart to see why we love someone and choosing to set aside our own desires for the sake of that person. Grace can be as precise as a moment of utter clarity, finally recognizing a long-sought decision or a direction to be taken.

While grace is forever respectful of the time we take to respond, this cherished presence doesn't always wait to be received and chooses instead to tumble into our lives right when we will most benefit from it. A retreatant told of being in a bookstore where she meandered around, looking for nothing in particular. A book fell off the shelf. She picked it up, put it back. It fell down again. She put it back. The third time the book fell down it hit her on the head. That did it. She bought the book, and it ended up changing her life by enabling a long-sought healing.

Many scripture texts reveal how grace thrives: the touch of Jesus' healing hands and voice in the gospels; the sudden blindness and subsequent conversion of St. Paul; the exquisite moment of Mary of Nazareth's yes to the angel's request; shifty, cheating Zacchaeus's quick climb down the tree so he could welcome Jesus; the courage of those standing beneath the cross at Calvary; Peter's heart-slicing remorse after his denial of the One he loved; and the intuition of the two disciples who decided to talk with the disguised Christ on the road to Emmaus.

Every turn away from our false self toward our true Self, each beckoning toward what is right, worthy, and good—this is where grace keeps on stirring, inspiring, urging, clarifying, and encouraging; it does so even when strong resistance pushes the door of our mind shut, even when our deeper self chooses unknowingly to be closed to this transforming presence. Joan Chittister, author of *In Search of Belief*, reminds her readers of how much can happen when grace is near:

> The Holy Spirit, God's energizing presence among us, the life force that drives us beyond ourselves, that whispers us into the great quest within, that makes life alive with a purpose not seen but deeply, consciously, stubbornly felt even in the midst of chaos, even at the edge of despair, sounds the truth in us that we are more than we seem to be. Life does not begin and end with us. There is more than we know, there is an electric charge animating the world at every level and, most of all, within. Holy Spirit suffuses all of life. . . . Holy Spirit is the great anti-gravitational force that calls us out of somewhere into everywhere, that keeps us moving toward, through, the black holes of life, certain that on the other side of them is light, waiting and wishing us on.

Yes, we *are* "more than what we seem to be." Right now, grace waits on the shelf of our lives, desiring to enter another part of our inner domain. When will this abiding gift be opened, received, and make a difference? Much depends on our awareness and receptivity.

Listen to the Echo

You stand on the edge of a canyon and you shout something. The world and the universe echo your own voice back, whether you shout "Yahoo!" or "Yee-haw!" That's how echoes work. What you throw out echoes your own energy back. "I love you." "Thank you, Creator!" "I am happy!" Such a small thing to consider but such a large thing to do. Which words am I throwing out to the universe today, and what will come back to me as a result?

~ Richard Wagamese

Across the valley in my heart, I can hear the loud voice of my unfinished self calling out, shouting worthless, worn-out messages that have resounded since youth. They echo back, reinforcing what is false. As long as I keep voicing this stuff, it persists in returning, influencing the patterns and fitful tempo of my inner self. The reverberations batter and taunt with harsh reminders of what has yet to be transformed, of the supposed impossibility of becoming the person of boundless love I have long desired to be.

At the same time, another message with a kinder tone resounds across my inner landscape, gaining volume each time I receive it with enough trust to believe in its authenticity. Supportive tenderness wraps around each syllable: "Remember you are loved. Your core self consists of lasting goodness." This message comes from the Compassionate One, echoing far louder than the sound of my incompleteness. The voice of this Being assures and reminds me: "Focus on the positive instead of harboring the negative. This will encourage and bring about the sought changes."

Echoes travel through an invisible space. In order for the vibrating sound waves to be transported to the receiver and return back to the sender they require an openness for this resonance. They also need enough stillness for the echoing vibrations to be heard. So the more stillness within and the less negativity that blocks my inner space, the more likely the positive voice of love will move back and forth in my life.

In *The Way of Paradox,* Cyprian Smith describes the universe "as an echo of God's voice" and then asks the question, "Why is it that a chamber is able to echo the sound made within it? Because of its *hollowness* and *emptiness*." Smith concludes that "standing within the Word, we come to understand and love properly the world which is the Word's echo. This is essentially a joyous understanding, because it gives us a sense of the *rhythm* inherent in things: birth and death, light and dark, growth and decline, gain and loss, breathing in and breathing out."

St. Paul reflects this rhythm when he describes Jesus emptying himself, refusing to cling to his divinity in order to enter into life as a full human being, as one who experienced both joy and sorrow, expansion and contraction, in his life and ministry. Paul precedes this statement by encouraging the community at Philippi to develop their "compassion and sympathy," to let the same mind be in them as it was in Christ Jesus. They are to have "the same love," and "do nothing from selfish ambition or conceit" (Phil 2:1–7). That's a high ideal, one that could only be accomplished by their own personal emptying process, clearing out their own echo chambers from whatever might hinder their love from reverberating in the lives of others.

This leads me to ask, "What if the words in my mind regarding people came flying back to me?" I certainly do not want the nasty ones about careless drivers to resound in my ears. Nor do I desire certain thoughts of *He should . . . She looks . . . I can't stand . . . What a . . .* , nor do I wish for utterances to come back to me with unreal expectations, quick dismissals, and acid antipathies. On a more positive note, I hope to repeat back to others the kind words of the Holy One that travel through my interior echo chambers: "I believe in you. I will never give up on you. I trust in your ability to grow. I care about you."

When I consider how Pentecost affected the early Christians, I envision the tempo of the Spirit's wild wind penetrating the hearts of those present, tugging loose any resistant hesitancy to give themselves fully to the gifts that the Spirit brought to them. Time and again these virtues echo through the Acts of the Apostles, demonstrating an amazing transformation in the disciples and assuring us that the echoing of the Spirit in their hearts was effective.

Most of us probably do not have a valley near us that's vast enough to carry a verbal echo, but we do have a passageway of communication in our minds, one that can send forth gracious and caring thoughts. And we have a heart chamber ready to sound forth with love. In choosing to live virtuously, we grow in reverberating the Spirit's gifts. If we listen for what echoes within ourselves, we increase awareness of the timbre in our actions. As our heart's attunement matures, harmony and peace filter through messages sent into the life of another, going out and returning—the endless cycle of an ever-expanding bond of loving communion.

The Splendid Voice tucked inside our hearts calls to each of us with grace-filled encouragement. These hopeful messages are meant to echo in our lives: "Love. (Love.) Believe in your goodness. (Believe in your goodness.) Be kind. (Be kind.) Trust in your ability to grow and change. (Trust in your ability to grow and change.) Peace be with you. (Peace be with you.) I love you. (I love you.)"

The Gift of Song

There is not a human being on earth who does not have a favorite song, lacking only somebody to play it.

~ Paulette Jiles

Every month I drive to Omaha, Nebraska, for a day or so of meetings at my community's motherhouse. The 260-mile round trip provides an opportunity for reflection, so all sorts of inner stirrings surface during the travel time. On one trip as I listened to Peter Mayer's "Singing a Song," a surge of zest swept through me. Soon I was singing along with the refrain. It was one of those moments like Brian Doyle describes: "When you are joyous a song comes to top off the moment and make you think the top of your head will fly off from sheer fizzing happy."

The more I sang, the more the melody released the excess burdens I'd collected over the past weeks. A song can do that and so much more. Music not only resounds externally; it tends to reach a unifying place within us where we humans experience unspoken connection. In the words of Erin Guinup who conducts the Tacoma, Washington, refugee choir: "Something magical happens when we sing. It's hard not to love people when you sing together."

In his reflection found on gratefulness.org, Brother David Steindl-Rast describes the flow of communion that music elicits in the human heart. He begins by quoting the poet T. S. Eliot, who speaks about music being received at a transparent level "that it isn't heard at all, but you are the music while the music lasts." Brother David then reflects on that statement: "You are the music. That means you vibrate with that music, and even though you might just be thinking of some flute music or piano music that you listen to, it's the music of the universe that you are vibrating to. It's the music to which this whole cosmic dance dances, and that flows through you—and that's your religious moment. And in that moment you know that you are one with all. You are the music while the music lasts, simply that."

How is it that music can instill such profound communion that some people even turn to song as death draws near? When I volunteered for hospice there were countless times when family and friends gathered by a bedside to sing to their loved one who lay dying. Although death would separate them physically, the songs they sang enveloped them in one another's heart-space and gave them comfort.

Unseen movement flows forth from music because these melodies consist of organized sound filled with vibrations. This is what reaches from our head to our toes when a song "comes alive" in us, whether that be a robust beer-drinking one, easy jazz, a soothing lullaby, a jubilant alleluia, body-swaying country, or toe tapping reggae. Raising our voices in song brings us together. The melody and meaning glide through and beyond our diverse personalities, religious beliefs, and political views. Singing with others allows a strong, unseen movement of common humanity to bridge the gaps. Patriotic songs remind those joining their voices that the goal and purpose of their country links them beneath individual disparities. (I fondly recall the moment when more than three hundred retreat participants in Truro, Nova Scotia, stood in a crowded hotel ballroom and thanked me by singing their national anthem. Even now, this remembrance of long ago creates a ripple of tender emotion.)

Music sustains hope in difficult times. Early gospel songs soothed the souls of oppressed people shackled to a life of slavery. These faith-filled hymns strengthened their resolve to not give up hope and gave them a way to communicate with one another when slave masters denied them this natural human connection.

The evocative song "Christmas in the Trenches" embodies the communion we share as humans when we move beyond what separates us. This song is based on a story from World War I; English and German soldiers lay in cold, muddy ditches opposite one another on Christmas Eve. On one side a soldier began to sing a

German carol. The English listened. Then both sides joined in singing "Silent Night" in their own language. Slowly the opposing forces emerged from their hideouts, moved cautiously toward one another, until eventually the singing gave way to sharing family photos, some brandy, and even joining in a soccer game.

Music like that often captures our spirit and lingers with us long after we hear it. A movie-goer mentioned how he kept humming the song "It's a Beautiful Day in the Neighborhood" after viewing the documentary depicting the life of Fred Rogers. When my friend Shelley traveled extensively in Asian countries, she told me that the song "It's a Beautiful World" wouldn't leave her alone. Researchers have termed songs that tend to stick in our heads as "earworms." Sometimes this "stickiness" becomes irritating. At other times, it provides reassuring companionship.

Kathleen Dean Moore tells of a "canoe song" that offered this kind of reassurance in *Holdfast*. She treasures this song because it reminds her of her beloved mother: "My mother sang the song softly, a lullaby, as she sat at the foot of the bed and my sisters and I drifted off to sleep. She hummed it as she dusted shelves and thought of other things. She sang it as she drove downtown, her elbow sticking out the car window, her purse on the seat beside her. When we were sick, or lonely, or homesick, this is the song she would sing to comfort us."

What is your song? What hums in you to accompany ordinary days, celebrate successes, release pain, soothe sorrow, encourage joy, or harmonize opposing voices when they tumble inside of you? Choose a song to lift yourself up when life weighs you down, one to ease the franticness of too much to do, and restore your confidence when it wanes. Find a song to hold you in remembered love when feeling bereft, a refrain assuring you of inner strength.

The gift of song reassures us that the Spirit of Music is right there, ready to create a symphony of joy out of what currently shapes our days. The melodies within our hearts can carry this energy through the Pentecost season and far beyond it.

How Do You Find Peace?

The more peace there is in us, the more peace
there will be in our troubled world.

~ **Etty Hillesum**

Shortly after the COVID-19 virus reached our state, an incident in
the supermarket troubled me. A stranger in the checkout line spoke
at length about the details of his work at a water bottling company
and how the pandemic was affecting his job, his worries of getting
his needs met, and the free lunches he applied for at two places. As
the man moved on, he lowered his voice and confided, "I'm afraid
of what people are gonna do, so I got two loaded guns in my house."
His comment unsettled me. Fear's ability to pounce on peace and
replace it with violence became more real to me that morning.

I wished I'd had the insight and courage to ask the stranger a
question that Pema Chödrön raises in her book, *When Things Fall
Apart*: "Every day, at the moment when things get edgy, we can just
ask ourselves, 'Am I going to practice peace, or am I going to war?'"
Fear in itself is humanity's friend, a natural response meant to protect our well-being. But when fear insists on taking center stage and
gobbles up peacefulness to replace it with hostility, fear changes into
an enemy.

Chödrön also writes in *Comfortable with Uncertainty* that instead of
"resisting our fears" we need to "get to know them well," to ask ourselves, "What happens when I feel I can't handle what's going on?
. . . Where do I look for strength and in what do I place my trust?"
That last question is a determining factor as to the choice of maintaining a foundational peace or succumbing to high anxiety when
fear arises due to an uncertain future.

Tara Brach's *Radical Compassion* includes a valuable meditation about releasing fears: "Let the fears you're carrying, the big ones, come to mind. And now imagine that you are holding them gently and respectfully in both hands . . . and placing them into the arms of the Divine Mother. It's not that you're getting rid of them. It's more like letting something much larger help you hold them. See if you can visualize and feel this. You might try actually cupping your hands and lifting them up."

Several other spiritual practices keep my mind and heart steering away from being swallowed by fear. One is to focus my mind and heart on the words of a prayer rather than on my fears, such as the Serenity Prayer, attributed to the American theologian Reinhold Niebuhr. The first three lines are most often worded this way: "Grant me the serenity to accept the things I cannot change, courage to change the things I can, and wisdom to know the difference." I also return to several lines in Nan Merrill's translation of Psalm 91, inviting the words to sink into my heart: "My refuge and my strength, In You alone will I trust. For You deliver me from the webs of fear, from all that separates and divides."

Even with these prayers, however, I have found myself captured by this imprisoning emotion. Fear became my enemy when it almost succeeded in convincing me to abandon an opportunity to visit the ancient ruins of Machu Picchu, the fifteenth-century citadel in Peru. Because I was scheduled to lead a retreat in Lima, it seemed possible for me to go early and visit the site. I had traveled alone in other countries numerous times and fear rarely grabbed ahold of me. But in this situation anxiousness took over my peacefulness as I wrestled with details of the trip, such as my ineptness at communicating in Spanish, personal safety, questions of lodging and how to travel to Cusco, the capital of the Inca Empire which is located at over 11,000 feet, plus how to locate the bus and train from there to the ruins. Just about the time fear would have squelched this awesome trip, I received a small but significant piece of information from the retreat coordinator. He told me of the little hotel he stayed at in Cusco and this led to my being able to tend to the other details that had generated fear. To think that I might not have had that marvelous adventure because of the bullying power of fear.

This powerful emotion affects us in a variety of ways. Some people allow fear to stir up hatred and violent responses, while others turn from fear toward compassion, nurturing inner peace and strengthening hope. Harriet Tubman's life demonstrates this. She narrowly escaped her captors when she fled from those who enslaved her. She knew full well the terror and danger of attempting such a heroic feat. Once she made it to free territory, Tubman could easily have settled into her newly found liberation. Instead, she confronted what terrified her and chose to deliberately go back into what she escaped in order to assist others to gain their freedom. This brave woman relied on trust in God and a resolute love as she repeatedly entered into extreme danger. Harriet Tubman risked almost twenty trips to bring more than three hundred slaves to the freedom she had acquired for herself. She did this, of course, with the compassionate help of other people working with the Underground Railroad, each one going beyond their own fears for the sake of others.

Our decisions to cultivate peace by confronting fear need not consist of such tremendous actions like Tubman's. What we choose to do might seem insignificant, but the outcome can prove to be surprisingly beneficial. During the COVID-19 pandemic I received a message from a friend doing this very thing. Joan wrote:

> On Pentecost Sunday I was feeling so troubled with the riots and violence that was being reported on the news. . . . To see George Floyd murdered so cruelly was horrifying. Here's what I decided to do. I rang my neighbors' doorbells and told them I felt distressed over the violence. I told them I am a Christian. This is Pentecost and we needed compassion and love. Would they like to join me at 9 p.m. when it is dark and social distance outside their homes with a lighted candle? Let me say, it was beautiful! Neighbors introduced themselves to other neighbors. My 21-year-old granddaughter and I stood outside with luminaries and candles and so many thanked me for suggesting this. I just knew I had to do something. It was very peaceful.

Trust overcomes fear. When fear lessens, peace grows stronger. When we choose to cultivate peace, we can also help others move away from fear. So why not corral those pesky fears and live more contentedly?

Hail Mary, Full of Grace

Hail Mary, full of grace,
full of Spirit,
full of questions and hesitation,
full of courage and receptivity,
full of eventual *yes*,
strength received for a journey
that became rougher
than you could have imagined,
full of more love
that you had ever dreamed.

Hail Mary, full of grace,
full of Spirit,
full of strength,
full of generosity,
full of the seed of Wisdom,
enough to carry the Child
who could change our lives
if we let him.

~ Joyce Rupp

June

This month invites us to reawaken our sense of wonder. Our five physical senses enable us to find sources of amazement in ordinary things such as feathers, faces, drab brown things, and the essential gift of our breath. When we look more closely at the world, we revive our ability to be awed. We see with increased clarity the intimate intertwining of ourselves with all of life.

The Voice of Unexpected Care

Dusky sky with darkness approaching,
just enough daylight to take my daily trek
through the silent woods into noisy traffic.
I move swiftly to complete the long walk
through the neighborhood of immigrants.

"One block to go," my old body sighs
as I reach the long hill sliding down
to my street. I prepare to descend as three
Nigerian boys make it to the crest. I turn
to them with "hello." Muffled returns.
But wait. The youngest, a small child,
wide eyes, round face, looks up and warns,
"Be careful. That's a *really* steep hill."

A child's concern for the white-haired woman.
Every joyful cell in my surprised heart expands.
The thoughtful words gladly attach themselves
to the deeper recesses of my vigilant self.
I bend toward him, express thanks for kindness.

In the following days, the child's voice
becomes the God-voice, caring and attentive.
"Watch out for those steep hills of your work.
Don't go too fast with your life."

So I slow my pace, quiet the rush, talk back
to the push inside trying to take over everything.
I remember the concerned message coming
from a thoughtful child near the top of a hill.

~ Joyce Rupp

One Drab Brown Thing

One pebble drab and brown
I keep and cherish.
Everyone should love
One drab brown thing.

~ Chan Sei Ghow

Why a drab brown thing? Why not something colorful, easily considered beautiful? Most people readily overlook the simple and nondescript in this world, whether human or non-human. "Drab brown things" do not meet the general assessment of what is worthy. There's a strong tendency to want the perfect, the unmarred. I noticed this recently in sharing a video on creation that opens with a newborn child. Someone seeing this child remarked, "Oh, that baby has such thick lips." Ah yes, a less than perfect body according to that person. I thought, *Does that make the child any less precious?*

Opinions and evaluations surface from an inclination to compare everything and everyone to some ideal notion held in the mind. So I like it that Chan Sei Ghow writes about cherishing a drab brown thing.

After reading this poem I asked myself, "What is the *one drab brown thing* that I value?" I searched my mind for what this might be, but nothing arrived. I then looked around my dwelling for something material and soon found the item. On my bookshelf sits a small llama with a baby attached by her side, an art piece created from dark, splintered wood. The figures have obviously been carved by an unskilled woodworker. But I value this little item that has been with me since 1976.

Why do I keep this drab brown thing? History. Memory. Connections. Looking at or holding this cherished item returns me to graduate school in Texas where I studied theology. During those years of early adulthood, my inner life took a leap into unknown territory, into expansive ways of understanding spirituality as it intertwines with life. During that time I also met my best friend who remains close to my heart to this day.

The worth of what appears unseemly or insignificant on the outside can be detected in a number of parables Jesus used in his teaching. Think of the minuscule, round mustard seed, the grain of wheat, a dirty coin buried in the earth, and tiny particles of yeast— and the lessons Jesus drew out of these. Who would have thought such big concepts might come from reflecting on these tiny bits of life?

Maud Dowley Lewis, a renowned Nova Scotian painter, is someone I never met personally but came to admire after viewing her life in the film *Maudie*. She was born with a physical disability that caused her to be hunched over and unbalanced when she walked. Rheumatoid arthritis gradually crippled her hands until every movement triggered pain. She was plain-looking, spoke slowly, and dressed in the simplest of clothes. From the outside, Maudie gave little indication of the magnificent woman glowing inside—an intelligent and gifted person who lived within a body that many walked past and thoughtlessly dismissed.

This kindhearted and forgiving woman existed in a tiny, disheveled, one-room, shed-like house with no running water or electricity. There Maudie began painting flowers on the walls to liven up the place. When the walls filled, she looked around for what else was available and painted on pieces of discarded wood. Thanks to the keen eye of a visiting tourist, eventually Maudie's art became known. Her reputation as an artist spread, and today her paintings are displayed in prominent art galleries.

Another woman comes to mind. In her later years of life my great aunt Ida Delperdang resided in a nursing home. I visited her whenever I could make the two-hour trip because she held a special place in my heart and history. She might have been considered to be "just an old lady," less than attractive due to a deeply lined face scattered with brown splotches. But to me, she was always beautiful. Her generous, loving spirit—combined with an ability to accept a life of poverty with graciousness—remains to this day one of my most cherished memories of someone with a golden presence.

Chan Sei Ghow's "drab brown thing" relates to the Asian concept of *wabi-sabi*. This concept values the imperfect and recognizes beauty in what some would want to discard or consider unacceptable. *Wabi-sabi* welcomes the well-worn and irregular aspects of material things, the chips and cracks that people, especially in the Western world, spurn. Seen with a *wabi-sabi* eye, what we might toss away actually holds considerable worth. Things such as a ragged childhood toy, a tattered owl feather, a faded photo, a frayed sweater with a missing button, an old book with pages falling out, a dying flower—each is appreciated for its history and intrinsic worth.

"The wish to improve life is real and attainable, but the desire for a perfect life—the perfect home, the perfect health, the perfect job, the perfect love, whatever it is—is the desire for something nonexistent," writes Taro Gold in *Living Wabi Sabi*. He recognizes the cultural influence: "Unfortunately, the hard-to-escape barrage of 'perfect' images in the media would have us believe otherwise. We all know the marketing mythology: Buy this perfect product, get that perfect life."

Accepting the less-than-perfect also applies to human relationships. "Perfect loves" rarely, if ever, exist. If we expect to find a faultless mate, a blameless friend, a colleague who never makes mistakes, a child with impeccable behavior, and a teacher or physician who knows everything, we will be disappointed. Everyone has imperfections, no matter how painstakingly careful he or she tries to overcome or hide them.

What is your drab brown thing that you value? Draw it close to you. It can restore your mental outlook and reset your heart's attitude.

Finding Feathers

My new song must float
like a feather on the breath of God.

~ Hildegard of Bingen

Do you wonder, at times, how it is that the Spirit moves in your life? I am often astounded at this engaging manifestation. Long ago, the appearance of feathers became a significant symbol for my inner journey. It all began in Boulder, Colorado, in 1993 when I was studying transpersonal psychology. One day I returned to my residence and found a white feather lying in the bathtub. Its presence astounded me. How could it have gotten in there? No window was open. No one else had been in the room. There were no feather pillows.

That experience stimulated an ongoing perception of spiritual stirrings in regard to finding feathers. I wrote about this in *Dear Heart, Come Home*: "A woman who practices Native American spirituality mentioned a feather as her key image. She described how the feather came from a creation myth that promises whenever two-legged creatures are on their spiritual path, following their passion, they will find a feather in their path." At the time I discovered the feather in the bathtub I was experiencing a lot of personal change, so this explanation resonated with me.

A feather can just be a feather, or we can allow its presence to open up a space inside of us that welcomes a connection, joining some fuller meaning for our life. When Jesus looked at the birds of the air, he did not simply think, *Oh, nice birds up there.* Instead, he saw a correlation between the birds and what he wanted to teach his disciples about not worrying. Jesus said, "Look at the birds of the air, they neither sow nor reap, nor gather into barns, yet your heavenly Father feeds them." This led to the message he wanted them to take from the sight of the birds: "So, do not worry about tomorrow, for tomorrow will bring worries of its own" (see Mt 6:25–34). In other words, trust God to take care of your lives. This essential message—from just looking up at some birds.

When feathers appear in my life, I most always find some sort of message that brings wisdom for my current situation. Last year I noticed feathers showing up everywhere at the time I faced some serious decision-making. A feather even came in the mail. A chaplain in the Northeast sent a shiny crow's feather to me as a gift, with the message, "Crow medicine has led me through many dark moments, as well as shown the light of hope amid the uncertain and unknown in my life." The arrival of that black piece of a wing encouraged me to trust the decision I eventually made.

Later that same month I recorded an amazing incident in my journal:

> So weary yesterday. After sitting by the woods overlooking the lake, I walked down to the beach where a large flock of terns had gathered. Feathers and more feathers. As I plodded along, I saw a long white one with a wide black edge—so exquisite that I picked it up to behold more closely. I thought to take it home with me, but something in me disagreed: "Leave it there." So I stooped over and gently placed the feather back on the ground. No sooner had I walked ten steps away than an astonishing thing happened. My tiredness completely vanished. I felt an instant resurgence of energy.

Upon sharing this with a friend the next day, she suggested, "Maybe it was not the feather but the action of letting go of the feather that restored your energy." Her keen insight helped me acknowledge it was time to let go of the heavy schedule of traveling for conferences and leading retreats, to gently lay down that way of life and move forward.

I treasure that unusual "feather moment" along with one of my most unusual discoveries of feathers. It occurred while I stayed in a small cabin on the northern shore of Lake Vermillion in Minnesota. After a day of writing, I left the quiet cabin on the cove to walk several miles along the shoreline of the lake. The owner of the cabin had mentioned on my arrival that their family had found a dead eagle on the western shore and gave a brief description of where I might find the bird. I had never seen an eagle up close, so my first day there I eagerly set off, determined to find it.

Keeping my eyes alert, I looked in all the possible places, but the remains were not to be found. I finally gave up the search and continued on my walk, surrendering to the fact that I was not destined to find that eagle. Later, when I turned around to head back to the cabin, I noticed a small path toward a sandy area on the shoreline and decided it was a good place to sit for a while and let my spirit sip in the beauty.

I walked to the small beach, sat down, and felt content as I gazed at the water. After about ten minutes I turned my head to the right and heard myself gasp—then I laughed. There, not eight feet away, lay the remains of the dead eagle. I had practically sat down on top of it. Only the feathered wings were left after wild creatures had fed on it, so this remnant also seemed significant in my discovery.

Eagle feathers are regarded as one of the most prized possessions of many Native Americans. Because of this bird's powerful strength, it symbolizes "trust, honor, strength, wisdom, power, and freedom." So I felt my being able to sit there by the feathers was a gift beyond measure. I smiled all the way back to the cabin, thinking of what a lesson the finding of those feathers held.

Not only was I given a blessing by seeing them, I also saw the connection to a spiritual teaching: When I gave up the search—let go of control and the strong determination to find the eagle—I was led directly to what I had been seeking. Not only that but I found the most precious part of what I sought.

I am obviously not done with feathers. (Or feathers are not done with me.) This summer they continually appeared on my daily walks. I spotted various sizes, shapes and colors—an ebony one in Texas, tiny pink in northwest Iowa, bright blue in Illinois, and at least five dozen on sidewalks during a week in the seaside town of Tremore,

Ireland. These findings assure me that more spiritual growth is waiting in the wings.

Gaze and Be Amazed

When we are filled with wonder
it is as if we've encountered the world
in all its beauty and mystery,
for the very first time.

~ Sharon Blackie

One misty autumn morning, on the kind of day that draws a person inward, I walked slowly around a quiet pond. As I strolled with ease, coffee cup in hand, I let my intellect take a vacation and my deeper self move into place. I deliberately stopped to be with the clear water, the dense woods beyond, and the steep, grassy hill. As I stood and gazed, each piece of nature took me in and transported my spirit into an easy peace. I felt a bit of the "thin veil" that Celtic lore uses to describe moments where the visible and the invisible mesh.

That evening I thought about the difference between *gazing* and *gawking*. Gawking hints of a negative connotation, such as prying or staring judgmentally. Sometimes gawking comes from simple curiosity about what is going on. Gawking, however, is radically opposed to gazing. When we gawk around in church to find out who's there and what they're wearing or when we drive slowly past an auto accident to see how badly the vehicles are damaged, that's an external approach of inquisitiveness. We intend nothing more than to glean information.

Gazing implies the opposite. It begins with an external look of open-hearted intent and ends with an internal response. Gazing involves soul-seeing. A silent bond gradually occurs when we gaze. John O'Donohue writes in *Anam Cara*, "When you really look deeply at something, it becomes a part of you." He relates the story of a journalist going to interview the chief of an indigenous tribe in South America. The journalist presumes they will spend the time conversing about the chief's life and beliefs. Instead, the chief sits quietly and gazes upon him. Gradually the journalist is drawn to return the gaze. They sit this way, gazing at one another for two hours. "After this time," O'Donohue concludes, "it seemed as if they had known each other all their lives."

That is the beauty of gazing. We come with an attitude of open receptivity. We slow down. We pause. This way of seeing with soft eyes and without judgment moves us to a quiet place of respect and awe. We can gawk at a person, a bird, or a flowering bush and miss the intrinsic beauty, but when we change our looking into gazing, that beauty comes home to our souls. It moves us toward a wordless knowing. The reality of the oneness we discover in gazing both humbles and inspires us.

Gazing is at the heart of contemplation. I was reminded of this in a letter I received recently. Mary Jane described "an ordinary drive, on an ordinary day" when she was intent on truly seeing the landscape. As she did so, she saw the ordinary as extraordinary. Mary Jane described "resting inside that moment." She told me that wildflowers on the roadside caught her attention and drew her to a halt. As she gazed upon the flowers, she "felt side-swiped by their loveliness." The result according to Mary Jane was that "all the nagging little concerns within me were whisked away."

Something similar happened two weeks earlier, only it was a person, not flowers, that drew me into soul-space. I was at a hospice facility visiting Marilyn, who was days away from death. As often happens, the weakness of her body was overtaking her. She barely had strength to whisper. I sat by Marilyn's bedside, gazing with kindness while she, with the luminescent radiance of the dying, looked into my face with such love in her eyes that I nearly crumpled. Deep, deep went our two souls. No words. Just a mutuality between us echoing the Great Love that embraces the world. In that space we met the divine in each other.

When is the last time you observed closely? When did you gaze with fondness on a child, spouse, partner, community or church member, friend, or colleague? When did you look past their crankiness and disagreeable habits to see the goodness beneath those irritations? How long since you paused to gaze at awesome storm clouds or the precious sliver of the moon as it waned?

I urge you to remember to gaze, not just a quick, winking glimpse or a brief nod of seeing, but to deliberately tend to what is visually before you. This action can draw you into amazement. When you do something so mundane and automatic as cutting your fingernails or toenails, pause to look more intently. Notice how beneficial and extraordinary these nails are in their ability to protect your hands and feet. Do not judge how they look; just take in the wonder of their existence.

As you eat, do you ever contemplate your food with awe, grateful for the journey the food has been on from its seed-form to its arrival on your plate? Each bite you move into your mouth holds a story of color, shape, density, texture—each is graciously ready to do its part to nourish and sustain your life once it is swallowed. (It's best to gaze lovingly at your food when you are alone lest your table companions grow concerned at your mental state.)

Revered Buddhist teacher Thich Nhat Hanh believes that "we have to look deeply at things in order to see." With this in mind, behold with wonder the patient you tend, the student you teach, the clerk you pay, the child you awaken, the people with whom you gather, the lawn you mow, the snow you shovel, the flowers you place in a vase, the dog you take for a walk, and the meal you prepare. Every one of these moments of seeing can be an opportunity to kiss the world with your eyes.

Gaze and be amazed.

First Breath, Last Breath

When we are born,
we are born into a relationship
with air, with breathing.
We are creatures into whom life is breathed.

~ **Gunilla Norris**

Right now you are doing something you are probably unaware of, but if you were not doing it, you would die quickly. You are breathing. The air you take in contains oxygen. As your lungs breathe this in, it fuels your existence. You cannot survive without this precious element. And every breath of carbon dioxide you exhale gifts the earth's vegetation with what it requires for survival. Stop and notice how this happens with each movement in and out of your breath. With the palm of your hand, feel the rise and fall of your chest or diaphragm. This life-giving pattern has been so much a part of you that you do not even know you're experiencing it unless your breath becomes shallow, or you become "out of breath" and have to pause to regain the natural rhythm.

What a magnificent pattern exists: give and receive, in and out, back and forth, fill and empty—establishing a unity of silent kinship with everything. The grasses of Peru's altiplano, rainforests in Tasmania, flowers in Ethiopia, prairies in central Canada, rice paddies in Vietnam, hanging vines in the Amazon—they are gifting us at this very moment as their out-going oxygenated breath circles the planet and floods the air we breathe. We are never alone, always in relationship with everyone and everything—breathing in and breathing out, joining and rejoining, receiving and releasing.

Gunilla Norris affirms this awareness in *Simple Ways: Towards the Sacred*: "With every inhalation we are given life. With every exhalation we must surrender that life, for another breath to be given to us. If we could fully enter the rhythm of this paradox we would live with immediacy, and be intimate with birth and death and life itself."

We enter into life on this planet with our first breath and leave with our last. In our fetal stage we relied on our mothers' breathing to receive the oxygen needed to develop our bodies. Researchers say that the transition of the baby leaving the womb and taking that first breath is complicated and "one of the most intricate things our body will ever do." What a gift we were given with our first breaths that jump-started our respiratory systems outside of the womb.

The last breath we inhale and exhale is equally phenomenal. I've become aware of this from the privilege of being with people in their final stage of dying. I've stood or sat next to the bedside, often-times holding the hand of the expiring person, looking and listening intently as his or her breath becomes increasingly shallow and less frequent. Slowly, slowly, the tempo weakens, with each inhalation and exhalation being further apart from the last. Then there is that breathless moment when the pattern ceases and the sound of life becomes "deadly silent." In that breathlessness, those gathered seem to hold their breath, wondering if there will be one more precious sound from the one who has just died. Always this moment of a final breath moves me deeply, knowing the person's soul has found freedom to depart.

Various verses of the Bible point to breath as our spiritual connection with divinity. The book of Genesis describes the Creator giving humans physical life: "breathed into his nostrils the breath of life" (Gn 2:7). Job acknowledges, "The spirit of God has made me, and the breath of the Almighty gives me life" (Jb 33:4). The prophet Isaiah assures his readers that it is the Holy One who "gives breath to the people" (Is 42:5). The psalmist insists that without the Creator's life in us, we would not exist: "You take away their breath, they die and return to their dust" (Ps 104:29). Jesus brings peace, unity, and spiritual vigor to his disciples by breathing on them and saying to them, "Receive the Holy Spirit" (Jn 20:22).

Physical breath. Spiritual breath. First breath. Last breath. On many levels we are breathing creatures. In his book *Silence*, Robert Sardello refers to an underlying kinship with all of life when he teaches about meditation and using the rhythm of the breath as part of this spiritual practice: "Rhythm is important as the practice itself because it brings us into harmony with the great rhythms governing the world: the rhythms of growth and death of plants, the rhythms of the movement of the planets and the stars, the rhythms of the tides under the influence of the moon, and the rhythms of all organisms. It joins us in harmony to the rhythms of the organs of our own body: to our heartbeat, breath, digestion, and the pulse of the blood, and to all of the organs. These rhythms, in turn, reflect the movements of the planets."

Not only do we have unity in the rhythms that Sordello names, but we also have a connection with those who have gone before us. Scientists assure us that the air we breathe into our lungs has circulated in Earth's atmosphere throughout the ages. We are inhaling the recycled air that our deceased relatives and anyone who lived on this planet breathed. We join in this universal and ancient breath uniting us through gentle breezes and aggressive gales.

Mark Nepo writes in *More Together than Alone*, "The Maori, indigenous people of New Zealand, have a custom of sharing their breath. They touch noses and take in each other's breathing and in this nonverbal way, affirm that their lives are connected. They do this every time they meet and leave each other. In sharing their breath, the Maori entrain their hearts and find their common rhythm."

We may not be touching noses and sharing our breath like the Maoris do, but we can still become aware of our communion with others through the precious rhythm of life pulsing through our lungs.

The Face Reveals the Soul

I am drawn to the face of another not because the other's face is different than mine, but because we share the same humanity and that we are sister and brother.

~ Ilia Delio

Upon reading a letter from a woman in her seventies, I was so inspired by what she wrote that I asked permission to share her message. "Rose" lives in a small town overseas. Each week she commutes by train for an hour into a large metropolis to spend a night and a day at her daughter's home, giving her daughter a break while she cares for her two children under the age of two. It is Rose's description of her journey into the city that stirred my soul:

> It is the opposite of what many do at my age. I take a commuter train, packed with people, often having to stand at least part of the way. Returning on Friday night, the train compartments are jammed with working folk going home, no air conditioning. My point is what this does to one's life of prayer. I am so conscious of humanity, of people in crowds and individually, a seething mass of people, busy, trying to earn a living. They are all God's children; we are all siblings.
>
> I pray the Our Father and wonder how is God's kingdom being built up by our activity; what is God's will for us. I pray for the people I'm sitting next to, for their work and families. I pray for the cab drivers, great philosophers and commentators, for the Uber drivers with stories from Somalia, Egypt, struggling-out-of- work-actors, Libyans, you name it. What a privilege to listen to their stories; they tell you such intimate things sometimes. So my spirituality

at the moment is not one of trees and seasons and nature, but of human beings in their diversity, their industry, their creativity. God gives us this drive, this vitality, looks with compassion on us all.

Rather than finding her strenuous trip a burden, Rose sees it filled with the remarkable bond of humanity. She envisions it as a spiritual adventure, one that unites her deep self with the hidden beauty of strangers pressing into her space. How grateful I am for Rose's reminder of the precious, divine life to be found in a congested commuter train.

I must admit that I did not think of standing in long supermarket lines, inching my way through large gatherings at a conference, or sitting in packed airline departure gates as a spiritual adventure; not until now. Rose graciously reminded me of the valuable approach I can take when being among a mass of people I do not know. I can relish the mystery, wonder, and strength of our common humanity if I turn my heart in that direction.

Irish author John O'Donohue relished the beauty he found in others. He wrote about this in *Anam Cara:*

> In the human face, the anonymity of the universe becomes intimate. . . . The face is the mirror of the mind . . . . Each face is a particular intensity of human presence. When you love someone and are separated from them for a long time, it is lovely to receive a letter or a phone call or even, in the silence of your own spirit, to sense their presence. Yet there is such deeper excitement when you return again and see the face you love; at this moment you enjoy a feast of seeing. In that face, you see the intensity and depth of loving presence looking towards you and meeting you . . . . The human face is the subtle yet visual autobiography of each person. . . . The face always reveals the soul; it is where the divinity of the inner life finds an echo and image. When you behold someone's face, you are gazing deeply into his or her life.

I've experienced what O'Donohue describes, but then COVID-19 wormed its way into our society and penetrated us so effectively that wearing masks to cover half of our faces became a key way to ward off being infected. I did not notice at first what this was doing to my experience of "the other," the persons I met on my daily walks or in my bimonthly visits to the supermarket. Several months after the pandemic struck, I came to the unpleasant realization that I was inwardly treating every stranger I met as a possible enemy, as "an infector." I had built a strong mental and emotional wall around myself. This realization alarmed me. As I reflected on how this interior change might have developed, I concluded that the wearing of masks tends to objectify others. Not seeing a person's mouth or smile, a central part of how that person reveals emotion, weakens the personal connection. It becomes much more challenging for the "face to reveal the soul."

Given this centrality of the face to the "knowing" of a person, it is not surprising that when Moses asks to see the face of God, he is denied this request. God responds, "You cannot see my face; for no one shall see me and live. . . . You shall see my back, but my face shall not be seen" (Ex 33:20, 23). Moses is given only the option of viewing divine presence from behind. It would seem from this revelation that to look upon the face of God would be extremely intimate, and Moses was not spiritually ready for this charged encounter, this profound act of communion.

This makes the well-known blessing from the book of Numbers 6:24–26 all the more significant when it is bestowed upon someone. This blessing asks that "the Lord make his face to shine upon you." Some translations word this as "the Lord turn his face toward you." While it might be assumed that this face turning toward us, this shining on us, comes from a divinity separate from the realm of humankind, it seems much more likely that it actually comes *through* human beings who carry this divine life within them.

The next time you find yourself in a throng of strangers, pause in the manner that Rose does. Look at the variety of faces. Open your mind and heart to their invisible stories and the journey of their souls. Find joy and solace in the recognition that a spirit drenched in divine goodness rests at the core of each person whose face you observe in the crowd. And then, rejoice that God's face *is* shining upon you.

Frail Beauty

Even the frailest beauty can enthrall,
soothe the rambling, noisy currents
of the soul's ever-changing tides.

Fragile beauty reflected in the deficient,
straggling among the frayed and worn,
trailing through unwelcome transitions,
sighing alongside bumpy terrain.

Sight of a limping doe with wounded leg,
the elderly face captured by creases,
a stormy sky with turbulent clouds,
the hollow tree felled by a gusty wind,
gingko leaves yellowing the grass,
exquisite in spite of their demise.

O Beauty residing within all that exists,
rinse my heart of its false perceptions;
reveal the clarity of essential splendor
veiled within what I consider blemished.

~ Joyce Rupp

July

Light fills these summer days of extended sunshine and brilliant displays of starry-sky nights. A similar, vast array of Light exists in the perpetual radiance dwelling within and around us. We turn toward the Light of our inner wisdom, regain trust in this guidance, and respond to the summons inviting us to dwell in the divine heart where we truly belong.

Eye-Kissing Light

eye-kissing light, the heart-sweetening light
~ Rabindranath Tagore

Sunlight, moonlight, starlight, artificial light,
the blessedness of these radiant beams,
taken for granted as much as one's breath
until the darkness refuses to make room.

Gray days smothering the heart with gloom,
long winter nights cloaked with thick tar,
shadows pursuing both mind and heart.
Oh, for the light to appear at those times.

Summer's welcome, strong sunny rays
laughing the soul out of her slumber,
kissing the eyes with lengthy days of light
and the pure joy of invigorating play.

Light, an expression of divinity's nearness
while darkness contains its own courtesy,
steeping hidden sparks like tea in a pot,
readying the soul for the taste of radiance.

The thin-veil moments of sheer surprise
when not only eye but heart is kissed
with unexpected revelation, chasing
the darkness away with one swift beam.

~ Joyce Rupp

Inner Radiance

A great force of energy moves deep in the earth, through the sea, and in the inmost heart. Whoever arrives at this place of inner radiance looks at the world from that one heart.

~ Paula D'Arcy

Bioluminescence. That's something I had not experienced until I joined a small group of women in British Columbia to travel by car in the twilight, across a small island, over wooded hills, and past grass-munching deer on the roadside. We arrived at a sandy beach on Tunstall Bay, flashlights in hand, and walked down a steep incline to settle beside washed-ashore logs. There we waited until darkness fully descended. When it did, into the water we went: the brave ones out into the cold ocean, the wimpy ones like me wading near the shore.

What I especially recall from that significant time is when Kathi first stepped into the water by a large boulder. She invited us to come to the stone's shadow where the water held the greatest darkness. Kathi swished her hand around in the water and immediately the movement caused it to bounce with sprinkles of light. "See," she said, "They're here. It just needs to be dark enough and have some movement to cause them to light up." And thus began my education within a magical evening of detecting starry lights in a totally new realm.

After Kathi's introduction, we moved further into the darkened water where tiny sparks of light glowed in the waves like fireflies. Zooplankton, tiny organisms that are unseen until they respond to movement by emitting a chemical reaction, created little luminescent flashes all around the part of us touching the water. What a marvelous moment—looking up toward twinkling stars in the ever-brightening dome of the sky and looking down toward the glowing sparkles in the watery universe below.

I thought about light of another sort that resides in humanity, a divine presence whose brilliance is much vaster than the ocean's depth and the sky's expanse. The little sea creatures prompted me to recall how we humans emit our own light. Our radiance hides not in ocean waters but in the fluidity of the soul and it, too, is detected through movement of some kind. Occasionally we catch a glimpse of this spiritual luminescence—all as real as little creatures releasing sparks of light in the water's darkness.

Most often this "movement of light" occurs when someone or something stirs the dimly-lit waters of our interior world and leads us to sense the presence of divine love. Along comes a person or event to part the waters with the "hand" of such movements as care, joy, laughter, comfort, forgiveness, understanding, and acceptance. The swift hand of love swirls through the midnight waters of loneliness, illness, hurt, sadness, and other emotions. A turning takes place within us. A radiance once hidden spreads through our soul's countenance, and we know we have been blessed. Our low-ebbed response to life changes when the sparkles of divine light move through our hearts.

Many are the times when light sails in and parts the darkened waters of my life. After a wearisome day clogged with demands, I walked at dusk and looked up to see the beauty of a rising full moon and felt bathed in peace. When I joined in a ninetieth birthday party for a dear friend whose Parkinson's disease crippled his mobility, I caught the jubilation in the light-filled presence of those who gathered. When I was with the family of my brother-in-law who was nearing death, sorrow crushed the hearts of those at his bedside—then came the words of his beloved spouse: "It's okay for you to go"—and a quiet, awe-filled light entered our hearts as he gained his freedom and departed for a new journey.

A powerful movement of this kind of spiritual bioluminescence occurred for Thomas Merton when he stood on the busy street corner of Fourth and Walnut in Louisville, Kentucky. This Trappist monk was granted an astounding vision: every person radiated light. In this flash of graced insight, Merton grasped the amazing truth that each soul emanates a sacred bioluminescence. After receiving that profound vision, Merton described his experience this way: "There is no way of telling people that they are all walking around shining like the sun. It was as if I suddenly saw the secret beauty of their hearts, the depths of their hearts where neither sin nor desire nor self-knowledge can reach, the core of their reality, the person that each one is in God's eyes. If only they could all see themselves as they really are. If only we could see each other that way all the time. There would be no more war, no more hatred, no more cruelty, no more greed. I suppose the big problem would be that we would fall down and worship each other."

"What if," Merton queries. What if I observed divine light shining from those whose philosophy, political stance, theology, and way of living opposes mine? What if I trusted that each person who comes into this world has "secret beauty" in his or her heart, no matter how heinous their crime or how defiant they are about what they have done? I don't think I'd be tempted to bow down to these people as Merton suggests, but my heart would be less recalcitrant, and my mind would hold fewer condemnatory judgments. I would want to look into the darkened waters within myself, swirl some kindness around in them, praying that a spark of light would guide my response when the light in others is hard to detect.

Like the night waters, our inner world remains hidden, but it can be glimpsed through sparks of love, beauty, kindness, wonder, and selfless service as they radiate from within us. When this happens, our lives shine like a constellation of divine love, a beauty to behold.

Trust Your Inner Wisdom

Your heart knows the way to go.

~ **Cynthia Bourgeault**

Within twenty minutes after settling into one of the comfortable cabins at Cedars of Peace forest in the hills of Nerinx, Kentucky, I looked out the screened-in porch, thrilled with what I saw. A spotted fawn on unsure legs wobbled nearby. The muscular mother nudged the baby from behind, apparently encouraging the slowly moving infant to explore her new territory. After some time, the doe walked ahead and turned to touch the nose of her newborn. The fawn then moved away to wander in the dense patch of grass near the cabin, eventually plunking down in a tall section of it. With her fawn safely hidden from view, the doe then left the scene.

As I watched the freshly-born creature snuggle in her safe place, perking her tiny ears up from time to time, I wondered when the mother would return. Five hours later, the doe still had not come back for her child. Worrying about the fawn's safety as I fell asleep, I thought, *What kind of parenting is that?* In the middle of the night, a bleating cry in the heavy darkness awakened me—the fawn calling for her mother. Both were gone in the morning.

After describing this scene to my friend Mary, she asked, "So, what do you think is the meaning of that?" I replied, "I don't know. I hope it will eventually become clear." Two weeks later the "message" arrived. Past experience has taught me that the discovery of insight and understanding requires a certain amount of patient waiting along with not trying to figure things out. Understanding ultimately surfaces only after stepping aside.

This letting go implies releasing a reliance on sources of perception based only on verifiable facts, the knowledge of certitude arriving through the physical senses, emotional responses, or rational mind. It's much easier to trust these pathways to personal insight and guidance than to trust intuition because intuition is more nebulous with its hints, hunches, and subtle nudges. A good portion of society emphasizes the rational—if it can't be proven, it can't be valid. Letting go of reliance on "being sure" includes a certain humbleness that comes with the territory of not knowing.

The cabin scene retaught me that not only does an implicit wisdom reside in myself and other humans, it also exists in creatures. How did that little fawn know to hide herself in the weeds? How did she understand the danger and necessity of staying put? Was there an unspoken code given by the mother? What really happened when the doe touched the fawn's nose? It seems to me that the doe's internal message told her she not only had to care for her fawn but also restore herself after giving birth. This mother knew she had to feed and rebuild her strength in order to nourish the waiting child. Some creaturely, instinctual wisdom existed within each of them.

Like the doe and the fawn, we have our own indwelling mystery and wisdom. Sometimes the wisest answers do not come from specific, provable "facts" but from an intuitive, trustful part of us. This reality can seem especially perplexing when we wander like a newborn fawn, wondering what direction to go with life's uncertainties, with issues such as strained relationships, tedious jobs, parenting tensions, religious misgivings, later-life diminishment, and societal gloom.

In recent years, the following quote has often been attributed to the famous physicist, Albert Einstein: "The intuitive mind is a sacred gift and the rational mind is a faithful servant. We have created a society that honors the servant and has forgotten the gift." Whether these are Einstein's words, I do not know. However, what led Einstein to his famous discoveries certainly had to begin with following his hunches, allowing himself to walk through a lot of unknowns before he arrived at what could be accepted with a logical, provable mind.

When something unnamed wells up inside of me, I know it's time to pay close attention, to not dismiss or set aside the unsettledness of what cannot yet be named. This welling up will lead to some sort of revelation that eventually shows itself not because of my self-congratulation of figuring it out and being assured of its verifiability but with the surrendering acceptance of trusting what I know deep down to be genuine inspiration.

As a writer, I've learned to be patient until indwelling insight is revealed. Sometimes I wait a long time for what is finally named. Eventually, this gift comes, maybe through an easy conversation with someone or in something I read. At other times, journaling, quiet meditation, or a walk in the woods frees the imprisoned words.

The book of Proverbs refers to Wisdom as an intimate, guiding presence dwelling in our midst. Wisdom is like the steady radiance of the North Star, a source that shines through the mystery of our everyday existence, guiding us toward our true direction: "Wisdom cries out in the street; in the squares she raises her voice. At the busiest corner she cries out; at the entrance of the city gates she speaks" (Prv 1:20–21).

The "city gates" signify the entrances to our interior being. There Wisdom cries out to us. With solitude, attentive listening, and firm trust, we move through these gateways to discover what this wise voice within ourselves desires for us to perceive. The guidance of divine Wisdom enables us to make good choices, live peacefully, and express the best of who we are. We are on the right track when we trust this inner companion's guidance.

Where Does My Heart Belong?

Love is where we've come from
and it is our destiny.

~ Daniel O'Leary

Last week I encountered an unusual creature on a forested walking path. I happened to look down and saw a tiny snapping turtle half the size of my palm. I almost stepped on the little creature because its camouflaged, mud-caked shell looked like a clod of dirt on the path. Its tiny head and feet were hidden under the shell, which led me to think the turtle was dead. When I bent over and lifted the turtle up to carry him to the side of the path, a slight movement told me the turtle was probably scared, not dead. I didn't want him to be smashed by a heavy foot or a biker's tire, so I laid the turtle down carefully in the grass. After I walked on about twenty feet a sudden thought stopped me. I remembered the small creek on our farm. Pregnant snapping turtles would come out of the water and go on land to incubate their eggs. They would dig a hole, lay their eggs, and cover them with soil for protection and warmth. I once saw turtles like the one I found on the path painstakingly making their way down to our creek after hatching. I said to myself, "That little turtle is just trying to find his way to the water."

With this memory I quickly backtracked and found the lost one, picked him up and walked a hundred feet to the edge of the lake. An amazing thing took place as I set the turtle down on the sand. At first the hatchling pulled his head and feet in tightly for protection. Then the head slowly came out and pulled upward, as if sniffing the air. The turtle wasn't looking at the water, but I soon realized he was actually getting a whiff of the moistness. He sat there for a minute with a puzzled look, then turned toward the water and moved as fast as his tiny feet would go. Into the lake he slipped, quickly out of view. If turtles have an experience of ecstasy, that probably best describes the moment of dashing into the water. I loved seeing what happened when he recognized home.

As I walked away from the lake, I kept smiling about the young turtle's recognition of where it belonged. Metaphors and parallels formed about my inner life. I wondered: Do I know my Source? Am I at Home? How often do I "sniff the air" and find where my heart belongs? How quickly do I move toward what brings the greatest sense of peace and well-being?

I thought of the countless things that distract me from heading toward the Source, toward the One Great Love where my heart knows I belong. I pondered what causes me to withdraw like the turtle when I fear what could be challenging or uncertain. Gradually a prayer formed and kept me bonded with the Holy One as I made my way around the rest of the lake.

Source of my life, Home of my spiritual heritage,
pick me up from the path of my fruitless wanderings.
Carry me back to you, the birthplace of loving-kindness.
Be tender with my fears. Draw me out if I tend to pull back.
When I get buried in the darkened corridors of uncertainty,
help me emerge from my mud-laden shell of confusion.
Reorient me in the right direction that leads toward you.
Show me time and again how to arrive where I belong.
Encourage me to eagerly seek your presence.
Remind me often that you are my Source and true Home.

Many are the times when I've lost a sense of where my heart belongs, when my life has filled with scrambled activity. Even when remaining faithful to daily prayer, my heart doesn't come home when my head constantly interferes by shouting out the next thing to be done. Only when I deliberately set aside what consumes my energy am I able to move to the waters of peaceful abiding, like that happy turtle eagerly finding the place of true belonging when it reached the lake.

Gunilla Norris assures us of the need to do this so we can find where we belong: "We need to abide and to settle. When we do, we will in time leave the ordinary way we rush, and enter the radiance of being in the eternal now where God is—and where we always actually are. It is there that we are meant to be. It is there that we live our true lives." Home is where contentment floods my spirit, where I can kick off my shoes and be at ease. I can be fully myself. I can *settle in*. I am at home, not just in my physical space, but within my own being.

In *A Testament of Devotion,* Thomas Kelley refers to this as "a wistful longing to slip into that amazing Center where the soul is at home with God. Be very faithful to that wistful longing. It is the Eternal Goodness calling you to return home, to feed upon green pastures and walk beside still waters and live in the peace of the Good Shepherd's presence. It is the life beyond fevered strain."

Kelley's reference to Psalm 23 reinforces the assurance of our belonging in the heart of Abiding Peace. When all seems lost and forsaken, when only fog and uncertainty cover the path ahead, when questions and doubts determine the mind's content, when cries of release from pain only grow stronger, when "home" seems far away, how comforting and supportive to recall the Good Shepherd's presence and guidance leading us to where we belong.

Like the little turtle searching for a home in the water, there is, as St. Augustine put it, a place in us that is restless until our hearts come home to rest where we belong. We move toward union with the divine ever so slowly, making our way toward this place of belonging, knowing in our hearts we are not yet fully where we are meant to be, not until we ease our way into the welcoming waters of a loving peacefulness.

Deep down inside we know the way. It's a matter of being intentional about heading in that direction and letting ourselves be picked up and carried when we lose our way.

Hidden Things

Hidden Seed
Deep in the dark soil of the earth,
Fertile Ground, Womb of the Night,
Bring us new birth.

~ Sara Thomsen

At the close of morning prayer, I looked up to see the sun beaming through the window, splashing the African violets with light. Having tended these plants for years, I gazed upon them with fresh eyes. I saw something not visible until that moment: the interior world of the thick leaves. They were fully transparent with the sunlight allowing me to see the veins and substance inside the leaves. It seemed I had been given a special privilege to look inside the hidden life of the violet where photosynthesis was taking place. Entering the violet's secret life, I understood that most of what I see in life only reveals the surface reality, whether that be of nature, humans, or creatures.

In her memoir, *Marrow*, Elizabeth Lesser writes about being a donor for her sister's bone marrow transplant: "I think about hidden things. Hidden life under the sea, under the ground, under the skin. The buried marrow in my bones and the secret stories in my heart. What are we supposed to see and hear, show and tell? Are things hidden for our own good, or is the human journey about going into the shadows and searching for the deeper truths about ourselves and each other, about life itself?"

A certain part of our lives will always contain buried mysteries we are unable to locate, but much of life holds revelations that could enliven and enrich our living if we took the time to delve more deeply into the shadows that Lesser mentions, to discover what inhabits that which is around and within us. Hidden parts of life can "bring us new birth" if we are willing to be explorers of this terrain and trust there is something to be discovered.

So many truths lie beneath the surface of who and what we encounter if only we are inclined enough to allow these to be disclosed. Whether this unveiling takes place with a verse of scripture, a pause to commune with a swallow building a nest, a group study on social justice, or a conversation where the heart of another yields unexpected revelation, there is always the possibility of our lives being affected in a way that alters us significantly.

James Martin, S.J., reflects on how much inspiration is to be gained by entering into the "hiddenness" of people in *My Life with the Saints*. He first ponders the unknown life of Jesus during his early years with Joseph the carpenter. Martin then leads the reader to persons whose lives are mostly unrecognized, the portion in them that contains much to be admired. He gives the example of refugees he worked with in Kenya, then extends this further: "The middle-aged unmarried woman who looks after her aged mother but whose sacrifices remain largely hidden from her neighbors. The loving parents of the autistic boy who will care for him for his entire life and whose heartaches remain unknown to their friends. The single mother in the inner city who works two jobs to provide an education for her children and whose tiring night shifts are still, after many years, a secret to her daytime coworkers."

James Martin concludes, "There are countless hidden lives of love and service of others. The day-to-day pouring out of oneself for God. It astonishes me how many of these people embrace their hidden lives of service with joy." Look around. Consider that a lot of the people you meet have their own "hidden lives," ones containing sacrifice and love at a level probably not visible or acknowledged.

George Washington Carver is quoted as saying, "Anything will give up its secrets if you love it enough. Not only have I found that when I talk to the little flower or to the little peanut they will give up their secrets, but I have found that when I silently commune with people they give up their secrets also—if you love them enough."

Loving enough implies being willing to be present, to approach and listen with kindly regard and humble curiosity.

Secrets hide in everyone and everything that exists. It just depends on where we want to look, what we desire to find, and how much we want to bring love into the search. How do we do this? How do we give anyone or anything our kindhearted presence as fully as possible? What might we find? There will be discoveries leading to an enlarged capacity for compassion, valuable insights for deepening and strengthening relationships, uncovered truths to heighten understanding, and revelations that surprise us with their power to transform our lives.

These hidden treasures might include a recognition of empathy found in regular visits to a friend with a serious illness; something as challenging as learning how to truly listen to a neglected family member by slowing the hurriedness pressing into each day; staying the course in a troubled relationship that eventually unearths a hitherto unknown source for resolution; giving enough love to our inner being in order to acknowledge the goodness that's always been there; or discovering renewed serenity coming forth from faithful prayer.

Irish author Sharon Blackie is at home with mystery and the accompanying result of living with some unknowns. Blackie writes in *The Enchanted Life*: "Mystery relieves us of the fiction that we know where we're going. It keeps us on our toes; it keeps our lives alive. The world, once again, declares itself to be a place of potentialities."

The reality of life's mystery with its "invisibility" and unknown dimensions serves as a catalyst for spiritual growth. Will we look deeply enough and long enough to discover what awaits birthing in the hidden potentials of our life?

Lighten Up

In one of the stars I shall be living.
In one of them I shall be laughing.
And so it will be as if all the stars
were laughing, when you look
at the sky at night.

~ **Antoine de Saint-Exupéry**

If you have ever had a time when you couldn't stop laughing, you know how therapeutic hilarity can be. Whatever tensions lodge in the body and spirit, they find release with this body-shaking enjoyment. Laurens van der Post offers a superb example of this in the scene of a cameraman named Duncan who was filming the life of the Bush people in the Kalahari desert. Not paying attention to where he was going, Duncan stepped back into a quick-grabbing thorn bush. "Instantly his hat was whisked off his head, the straps of his light meter snatched out of his hand and his clothes held tight by the finely curved thorn."

While most of the Bantu servants managed not to laugh out of politeness, Dabé erupted with laughter. "He went head over heels backwards to lie wriggling with merriment in the sand. During the rest of the day, whenever he remembered the incident again, the laughter would bubble afresh in him. It was wonderful to hear and to see his whole face joining in, the skin breaking all over into innumerable little crisscross creases and folds of the most endearing kind, and his body shaking with the spasms of sound breaking out of him."

When the events of life weigh heavily upon us, it is time to have some of Dabé's joy. Not all stressful situations call for laughter. Some are entirely too painful and serious. But much of what leads to apprehension can be eased with a bit of laughter. My friend Joyce Hutchison, director of our city's first hospice, taught me about the value of humor. I could never be with her for very long without both of us chuckling about something. When I first began as a hospice volunteer, I was alarmed to hear Joyce laughing at the bedside of a dying patient. I wondered if that was appropriate, but when I saw the joy on the man's face, I understood what Joyce taught: "We live until we die." Laughter is a part of life. It lifts the spirit and lightens the load, even when we're dying.

After Joyce retired, she volunteered her services at a retirement center. Because older people tend to have high blood pressure, she went regularly to check on them. She was concerned about the "doom and gloom" atmosphere when they gathered in the room. One day she encouraged the elders to laugh more as a way to ease their anxiety and worry. The next time she arrived they were seated in their usual chairs, waiting for her. As soon as she walked in, they all began laughing "Ha, ha, ha!" to assure her they had gotten her message.

Not long ago, I discovered the positive benefits of laughter when I taught a seminar for chaplains of a large health care system. I enjoyed both their ethnic and religious diversity—men and women from Kenya, Colombia, Poland, Ireland, Ukraine, India, Canada, Mexico, and Central America. The staff decided to have a fun time after lunch to encourage the chaplains to relax because their work tended to deplete them emotionally. They invited the group to play charades.

Playing charades turned out to be an awakening event for me, as well. I learned a lot by observing the group. A number of the chaplains had never heard of the game, but they eagerly entered into it. Each table was given a bowl with slips of paper containing titles of my books. One person was to silently act out the title and the rest of the group was to guess what it was. The previously sedate chaplains came alive. What a hilarious time they had. I looked to see a rabbi dancing around the room with his hands held high in the air, trying to act out *The Cosmic Dance*. Another person was attempting to get people to recognize *May I Walk You Home?* by walking arm-in-arm with someone. Laughter erupted everywhere with easy delight on the chaplains' faces. Later that evening I reflected on the day and thought about what a gift laughter is for us human beings. When we laugh, our spirits seem to grow wings and temporarily carry our burdens far away.

Laughing at ourselves is a healthy experience, too. I had an opportunity to do this a few weeks before the chaplains' seminar. When I was with a group of ministers, I spoke with them about our "personas" and how difficult it is to discover and claim more than who we think we are. At the break, a minister told me he had a story about "personas" and proceeded to tell me about a time in the airport when another minister pointed out two Catholic women religious to him. He was surprised she recognized the women as sisters because they wore nothing resembling a habit. He asked her how she knew. The minister replied, "Oh, that's easy: "Hair too short, skirt too long, shoes too flat!" I laughed heartily as I looked at what I was wearing. Ah, yes, his comment was right on target.

Actor Alan Alda commented in an interview, "When you laugh, you're vulnerable. You're opening yourself up. You're not protected. That's why a lot of executives don't laugh much, because they think it gives up their strength. But you gain so much through vulnerability. You let the other person in, and that brings us all closer."

So, let's be sure to laugh. We will be healthier, draw closer to each other, and have a good time doing so.

Love Lights the Heart's Lantern

Come, Incandescent Love, ever aglow,
ignite the silent wick of happiness,
abide by the hearth of discouragement,
revive the waning fire of contentment.

Come gliding in on your golden wings
when love sputters, dims, and flickers;
surround the lantern, breathe into it,
until the light leaps into a strong flame.

Radiant Companion of nomadic souls,
light their way home to inner peace;
emit sparks of joy on gray-filled days,
guide unsure steps on the rocky paths.

Let every glimmer in the midnight sky
be a welcoming beacon of confidence;
arouse the faint light of the heart's lamp
into a fervent flame of union with you.

~ Joyce Rupp

August

All of life can be our teacher if we choose to be open to everyday experiences. There we realize more about who we truly are and grow in accepting both our positive qualities and undesired flaws. When we learn to balance joys and sorrows that inevitably visit us, peace of mind and heart ripen in us like the fruits and vegetables in August gardens and orchards.

Stolen Lemons

Silent yellow fruit, ripe and ready,
asking for nothing,
not from the one who steals,
not from the one with plans to use.

But the one anticipating
juice and joy
comes away with empty hands,
robbed of hope and expectation.

The basket of fruit sits vacant,
while the basket of her heart
fills with unbridled anger,
knots of hardheartedness
sealing the mind's gate,
determined to do one thing only,
get those lemons back,

before her heart turns as sour
as the lemons she seeks.

~ Joyce Rupp

After entering a retirement residence, I found notes posted through-out the halls: "Bring back the lemons you took from the dining room. They were mine. I planned to use them." I laughed at the silliness of the message. This initial response followed with sadness at the possibility of someone being upset by a few missing lemons. Later on in the day I pulled in that judgment, realizing I have plenty of my own "stolen lemons"—those insignificant things I fret about and give way too much of my concern.

Discovering Our Teachers

To see requires learning to live awake. When we realize this hallowed way of being in the world, our teacher will no longer hide. When we begin to live awake, we will see teachers everywhere.

~ Macrina Wiederkehr

Have you ever heard of an Upaguru? Mark Nepo's *Seven Thousand Ways to Listen* introduced me to this term: "In Hindu, an Upaguru is the teacher that is next to you at any moment. This is not limited to a person." So, an Upaguru can be anyone or anything that shows up and brings an awareness that influences and teaches us something for our growth.

Upagurus usually arrive unannounced and unexpected. Probably you have had numerous occasions to learn from them. I certainly have. One of them visited me when I happily ensconced myself in a one-room cabin on a knoll above an expansive lake. My eyes relished the delightful view from the full-length windows on three of the cabin's sides. I plunked my canvas chair in front of one of the windows for morning meditation, prepared to sit in the stillness, confident of the Spirit's guidance.

It took a while before the Upaguru revealed itself. As often happens, this teacher had been there all along, almost directly in front of me, but my senses had to become alert before I could acknowledge its presence. There it was: a healthy, young birch tree. Midway down the trunk dangled a completely dead branch, still tightly affixed to the tree. Even though death was firmly fastened to the young birch, at least a dozen healthy, green-leafed branches stretched outward from other parts of the trunk.

The longer I sat and gazed at the birch tree, the clearer the teaching became: "Live with the brokenness and keep on thriving. Let the deadness of the past and the ineptness of the present remain if it must, but turn to what holds the possibility of constructive growth. Choose to focus on what matters. Do not allow your own or another's resentment, disappointment, hostility, or other negativity to consume the nutrients that feed love. Be a conduit of positive energy just as the trunk of this birch tree is a conduit of life for those green-leafed branches."

Hope swept through me as I recalled growing beyond tough situations when the storms of life whipped around me. In spite of those distressing circumstances that dangled like dead branches in my heart, I found the graced resiliency to not give up. I then recalled persons who are currently responding to much harsher storms than I've ever endured. They are receiving cancer treatments that wipe out their energy, tenderly caring for a partner with Alzheimer's, working as a single parent with two emotionally impaired children, and bearing heart-aching grief after a loved one's suicide. Like the young birch tree growing healthy branches, each person continues to generate patient kindness and generous compassion despite his or her difficulty. Each one remains life-giving even though an unwanted difficulty hangs onto their lives.

If I could summarize the teaching I received that day, it would be this: Being totally absorbed with an ineffective part of life results in a narrowing of vision and having a constricted heart. Releasing that focus and opening up to the possibility of growth does not deny the dangling branch. It simply lets it be and nurtures what still produces life. For the human heart, wounded yet resilient, much remains. It can be touched by life-giving grace and make room for quiet joy.

While Upagurus often reveal their unforeseen lessons through nature, they also sit on the pages of scripture when I am ready to take notice. Yesterday my teacher came through the story of four dedicated men determined to have their paralyzed friend be healed by Jesus. "So many gathered around that there was no longer room for them, not even in front of the door," so these creative guys climbed up on the roof, cleared an open space, lifted the heavy stretcher up there, and lowered down their friend (see Mk 2:1–12). This action embodies selfless love. The men not only gave their time, energy, and care, they also risked having the roof cave in and result in physical injury to their friend, themselves, and those in the house. Their unwavering compassion teaches me to act out of that type of unselfish love, too.

A totally different Upaguru arrived one winter through a song I was listening to on an eight-hour drive alone in my car (my little hermitage on wheels). As I was enjoying Sara Thomsen's song "Canticle of the Feathered Ones," something caught my eye. I looked to the right and saw what appeared to be a patch of large snowballs. But then the "snowballs" moved, revealing a hundred or more snow geese with their wings wrapped snugly around their feathered bodies. My heart leapt with delight at their presence.

No sooner had I passed the geese than clouds of migrating blackbirds descended from the sky, almost completely covering a small meadow. I rejoiced, thinking of the countless small hawks on treetops I'd noticed earlier in the day. The exquisite synchronicity of those feathered ones being present while I was listening to the song taught me anew how unexpected pleasure makes an entrance. Upagurus are everywhere—but only if I actively connect my inner and outer worlds by being attentive to my surroundings.

"God is an infinite secret hiding in the open," writes Mark Nepo. The divine Spirit does truly move through our lives, nudging us to be vigilant and receptive to our teachers. Those blessed Upagurus constantly bring us lessons for how to enter and enjoy the fullness of life, even when a dead branch hangs onto our hearts.

Lessons of Life from a Sunflower Field

in everyday the blessing of weather
offering change
a constant passing
of life into death
and back again

~ bell hooks

Growing up in rural northwestern Iowa, one would expect I'd be familiar with sunflower fields, but no one in our area grew them. After a friend mentioned visiting the colorful fields in a nearby state park, I was intrigued. I went there a week later but arrived too late. Instead of a stunning view like a Van Gogh painting, the desolate fields reflected Samuel Beckett's play *Waiting for Godot*. The once brilliantly colored flowers had matured quickly with the extreme August heat. Now the faded yellow and brown tattered heads hung downward on bent stems, reminding me of the curved-over woman in Luke's Gospel with her head reaching toward her heart. I almost turned around and went home but something inside of me insisted on my getting out of the car to look more closely.

Once I walked into the field, disappointment turned to wonder. I never knew how large the sunflower heads could be, some eight inches across. Because of such abundance, the seeds' weight forced the stems to bow and stoop. I noticed flocks of goldfinches deliriously feeding on seeds that spilled out from sunflowers now transformed into nourishment, seeds giving away the enrichment of their summered lives.

As I left the field, I felt urged to return. I sensed I had more to learn from the surrendered sunflowers. Two days later I came back, ambled slowly through the field with the heavily drooping heads brushing against my body as if to say, "Listen, we have something more to tell you." And speak they did, about the necessity of release, the ability to freely give away what had been their glory. I understood that the dying field held not only a harvest of fulfillment but the acquiescence of what it contained, an acceptance of giving away what was never theirs to keep.

Each day the plants became receptive vessels of transformation, allowing the roots to draw forth moisture and pass nutrients through the stems and into the flowers. They stood in the scorching sunshine and endured torrential rainstorms. They accepted the withering of their beauty and the subsequent formation of the seeds. In the end, those seeds could not be kept, no matter how diligently the plants had nurtured them into maturity.

My thoughts became absorbed in how much it cost the plants to bring forth this rich harvest. Those heavy, drooping heads replete with ripened seeds spoke to me of personal diminishment, of all sorts of loss bound to come sooner or later—loss that weighs down the heart with sorrow, presses on the mind, and pulls away from us what we hold dear. *Whatever we grow by our work and prayer*, I thought, *we cannot hoard it to ourselves, and we may become bent over in the doing of it.*

This costly transition does not only happen to individual persons. Societies and organizations also experience seasons of bending low. Dying comes before rising. Death arrives before new birth. Few want to accept this reality. But accept it or not, this pattern shapes how growth typically occurs. Unable to hold their heads high any longer, the sunflowers bowed to the way life naturally unfolds—the ageless pattern of life, death, rebirth—and taught me anew that I, too, wend my way through this configuration, slowly bending the stem of my life, allowing my head to reach my heart, accepting the pattern in order to have peace.

I thought I was finished with the sunflower field but now I know I will return one more time. Before the snow flies I will go and stand in the field of stubbles. With the harvest completed, I'll view the empty field with its riches given over to a voracious combine. I'll stand there absorbing the truth of the sunflowers' generosity.

I will take in yet another truth: the period of emptiness following the release, when what has grown and matured eventually departs, leaving barren soil to rest in winter's fallowness. I will wait, then, for the coming spring when the field will again be filled with sprouting seeds alive with a new pattern of growth, liberation, and fulfillment.

After the above observations went forth in an August newsletter, messages poured in from readers who identified with the lessons I found in the sunflower field. A wife sitting vigil with her husband in hospice care found strength to accept his dying process. A daughter mourning her mother's passing recognized a similarity with the sunflowers: "a perfect picture of how she was bent low in her later years after blooming so brightly for so long. How she continued to give to and nurture so many people with whom she came in contact. Her seeds have been devoured." Several persons spoke of how their deceased loved ones had appreciated sunflowers and their surprise when these plants often showed up in the most unlikely places after their loved ones' deaths, such as "at the center of the lawn" or "in a planter of herbs."

These poignant communications assured me that others resonated with what I found to be meaningful: life, death, and rebirth as the natural pattern of development. This reality connects to what Rosemary Luling Haughton assured her readers: "Transformation is part of the nature of reality because nothing is static; change goes on all the time, in people and plants and rivers and mountains and society."

Wherever our lives currently reside within that pattern, we can take comfort that we are not alone. Others join us in this great adventure of the human spirit. What strength and encouragement there is in knowing this to be so.

A Delicate Balance

> When we cover over our innocence and purity, our vulnerability and tenderness, we lose sight of our essential being. Our identity becomes linked to our ego space suit, and we forget the gold.
>
> **~ Tara Brach**

At the hair salon a boy of eight or nine years paced in front of the reception desk. He spoke loudly enough for everyone to notice: "When are we getting out of here?" The quiet smiles of those sitting around the room encouraged him, so then the boy announced, "I have patience problems." A few minutes later, the smiling response of his audience faded when he added matter-of-factly, "And I have autism, too." As I left there I thought about that boy and of a small girl a few months earlier who walked with her mother into a department store. The pouting girl resisted her mother's hand, deliberately lagging behind. She made a grousing comment I could not detect, but I heard her mother respond, "Oh, it sounds like you have anger issues again."

Our society encourages children to be aware of the thoughts and feelings that prompt their behavior and to identify what activates them. While youth can grow positively from this approach, at the same time I wonder if children may unconsciously be learning to identify and limit themselves by descriptions attributed to their behavior. Hopefully adults offer assurance of a deeper stream of uniqueness within the youth, one that carries more than the child's illness, shortcomings, or physical disabilities.

Wayne Mueller recognized this need for balance in how adults assess themselves. In *How Then Shall We Live?* he refers to the affirming encouragement Jesus gave his disciples, "You are the light of the world" (Mt 5:14). Mueller then goes on to reflect, "We have been reluctant to say 'I am the light of the world,' and more likely to confess, 'I am neurotic; a child of an alcoholic; a manic-depressive, a codependent; an adult child of family dysfunction; an over-achiever; an incest survivor; an addict,' and so forth. While these names may be accurate in some particular way, tracing the legacy of early trauma, they are limiting and inadequate in the largest sense. They cannot describe our true and deepest nature."

How subtly this limited identity slips into a person's inaccurate portrayal of self. I recall a friend whose struggle with hyperactivity and restlessness went on for years. Finally, he learned through psychological testing that much of what he experienced was due to ADD, attention deficit disorder. This knowledge relieved him of the stress and guilt of trying to complete tasks in a timely and orderly manner. However, from then on he explained his diagnosis by saying, "I'm ADD"—not that he suffered *from* ADD but that he *was* ADD. My friend equated himself with the illness itself. He lost sight of the larger part of his being that contained a magnanimous compassion and exceptional creativity. He strayed from remembering his essential character, his *true and deepest nature.*

Think about your response when asked to speak about who you are—not what you *do* but who you *are.* If you were asked to identify yourself in a way that includes your physical, mental, emotional, and spiritual self, what description would you use? Do you believe your "you" consists mainly of the categories you've placed yourself in? Have you been able to view the larger and deeper part of your being where your finest, enduring qualities reside?

In a sense, each of us is a prospector at the stream of life, searching for nuggets of gold. Before we discover the treasure, there's a lot of digging through dirt and stone, sifting through what appears to have little worth. If we focus only on the mud and grit, we gradually lose heart and forget there's something of value to be found within that mess of murky gravel and gummy clay. We dare not forget that our greatest worth may very well reside in what appears to be an obstacle or hindrance. The aspects of self we'd like to get rid of often provide the means for teaching us about our golden essence.

We do not live in a neat and tidy world, whether interiorly or exteriorly. Each day brings with it the challenge of balancing our belief about self. We cannot afford to identify ourselves solely on a stereotyped category or typology. Growth in becoming our truest self requires naming and claiming *all* of ourselves. At the same time, we do not allow what we see as the limited part of ourselves to be an excuse for poor behavior, lack of responsibility, or a limit of our desire to continue becoming more whole.

Our ordinary lives allow for plenty of opportunity to discover and balance who we are and how we are as we grow in knowing more about our goodness. Margaret Silf, retreat leader and spiritual teacher, assures us of this:

> It is within our daily experience that we most learn who we are, and also how we are most drawn to live who we are by the way we are with others. . . . I once heard that "truth is delivered to us daily, fresh-baked in ovens of our own experience." Try dwelling on the picture these words evoke for you. Try making friends with your "oven"—your everyday experience. Reflect on the possibility that the walls that seem to enclose you, the heat and frenzy that seem to stifle you, and the delays and frustrations that seem to hold you back may be the very means of revealing the truth that is already in your life.

Let us not define or identify ourselves by our illness, our limitations or unfinishedness, our "disorders" or disappointments. Golden nuggets reside within our stream of self. As the western prospectors used to say, "There's gold to be found in them thar hills." Let us move to the interior of our being and claim the wealth that is ours.

Accepting the Flaws

"What's your best discovery?" asked the mole.
"That I am enough as I am," said the boy.

~ Charlie Mackesy

As I prepared to call my friend and ask her to look for an item I'd left behind on a recent visit, I chided myself, "Here I go again, not being observant enough." I stood there for a moment, phone in my hand, while a long list of stuff I'd inadvertently forgotten at other places briefly waved an accusatory finger. Over the years, that list has grown long enough to fill an oversized suitcase or two. Some overlooked items I distinctly remember: a cherished T-shirt in France, a bathrobe in a North Carolina motel, a billfold in northwest Iowa, and a favorite water bottle in Illinois. It seems no matter how carefully and completely I check before leaving a place, invariably something remains behind.

This part of my personality I do not like, but no matter how much I try to change, I continue to be somewhat of "the absent-minded professor" when it comes to collecting every personal article. This situation began long before aging's natural process of a sluggish memory kicked in. I'm either in a hurry, too preoccupied, or not sensate enough to notice what's right there in front of me—even when I've painstakingly checked that everything is with me. Though I find this flaw humbling, I've eased up on berating myself for this inadequacy and learned to accept it for what it is: a blemish that intends to hang around.

Everyone has some sort of flaw that occasionally flails them or affects others adversely. Some persons lose patience easily. Some cannot recall people's names, overdo it on tending to details, or always arrive late for events. Others do not have a sense of direction (even with GPS), blurt out opinions too quickly, or can't carry a tune. While accepting our flaws, we do what we can to not allow them to roam freely or create distress. These aspects of ourselves can cause damage to valued relationships and endanger jobs. My own forgetfulness has robbed time and energy from people, like my friend who had to ship my calendar overnight, or my sister who had to drive twenty miles to deliver my overlooked bookbag.

It's good to remember that our flaws do not define us. We consist of much more than these imperfections. I rediscovered this truth at the farmer's market where I found a table with sacks of golf-ball-sized peaches. "Grown in Iowa?" I dubiously queried of the farmer. "Oh, yes," he said, "they're very sweet. But be sure to peel them." Good advice. The skins were mottled with scurvy-like spots and tiny brown pocks. I decided to take the risk and bought a sack home. To my happy surprise, they were the juiciest, tastiest peaches of the summer.

If I had judged the peaches from the outside, I'd never have known what was on the inside. The same is true with humans. If I can get beyond the "peel," beyond what seems bothersome or offensive, and go deep enough in my search for understanding and acceptance, I find we are more alike than different. A basic goodness resides at our core.

In teaching the Focolare community which she founded, Chiara Lubich addressed the presence of personality blemishes: "We had said we wanted to see only Jesus in our neighbor, to deal with Jesus in our neighbor, to love Jesus in our neighbor, but now we recall that a neighbor has this or that defect, has this or that imperfection." Lubich recognized that the longer we know ourselves or someone else, the more clearly both our goodness and flaws float to the surface. In acknowledging that none of us is perfect, we can accept that everyone has certain pesky rascals that try to trip us up.

With this in mind, we do not judge others harshly for what is less than their best self because we know that our own shortcomings can keep us from being our best selves, too. Alongside that, there resides a bigger portion of who we truly are. We can say to ourselves, as did the poet Walt Whitman, "I am larger, better than I thought. I did not know I held so much goodness."

If we accept the totality of ourselves, including the things that sporadically bump us off track, we will have greater peace. This wholeness came home to me again one autumn when I watched fluttering maple leaves in a sixty-second video by photographer Jim Brandenburg. I was intrigued with the contrast between the close-up shots in which each yellowing leaf revealed a blemish of some sort, and the wide-lens view of these same leaves showing a dazzling forest. In the extensive view, none of the blemishes stood out—even though each leaf held an imperfection such as partial discoloring, a ripped edge, or a dark spot. When seen as a whole, my eyes beheld sheer loveliness. When viewed as individual leaves, I had to look more closely to appreciate the beauty.

Like those autumn leaves, we look inviting at a distance and yet can appear a bit tattered and torn when viewed close-up. Then the defective holes in our ideas and the ragged edges of certain behaviors reveal themselves. Whether with individual maple leaves or with individual humans, when we stand objectively and gaze with kindhearted eyes, we marvel at the goodness and the ability of the human heart to sustain and comfort others. The flaws within each person dissolve in the beauty of the whole, a vibrant hue of kinship and solidarity.

In Peter Mayer's song "Japanese Bowl," he refers to goodness and imperfections both containing their own blessedness. He bases his song on the Asian art of "kintsugi, in which the artist seals cracks in pottery with gold, demonstrating that something of beauty exists within the incomplete or flawed object. Mayer sings, "I'm like one of those Japanese bowls. I was made long ago. I have some cracks you can see. See how they shine of gold."

Walt Whitman was right. We are larger and better than we thought. We hold so much goodness.

Choosing Equanimity

> Peace is not about moving away from or transcending all the pain in order to travel to an easeful, spacious realm of relief; we cradle both the immense sorrow and the wondrousness of life at the same time.
>
> **~ Sharon Salzberg**

Every once in a while, my heart swells with gratitude because of a wise and courageous decision someone makes regarding their future, a decision that leads to tranquility. I am left with not only amazement but with the hope of being able to do likewise if I am faced with something comparable. I felt this way when my close friend of more than fifty years called with distress in her voice. She was trying to make the "right choice"—whether to have surgery for the cancerous tumor rapidly growing in her brain or to let it be. With the exception of the surgeon who indicated "it will prolong life for a while but it's just a matter of time," the relatives around her kept urging my friend to go ahead with the surgery, to endure the radiation and extensive chemo to follow, "to tough it out." This choice would give my friend a bit more time—but it would not save her life.

After listening to my friend's tearful voice and the explanation of what she faced, I asked just one question: "Deep down, when you go to your core, what decision will most lead you to peace?" After a short pause, she said, "I don't want the surgery. I'm not afraid of death. I just want to go home and accept what is." A day later, after choosing to forego surgery, my friend returned home with a more tranquil spirit, one that basically persisted during the five months of her remaining life. Of course, she had to renew and restore that serenity as her body experienced severe transitions, but each time she managed to return to and retain a sense of rightness about her choice and a peacefulness about her approaching death.

Most every day something brings with it the possibility of a disturbance. These "somethings" are not always the giant type that confronted my friend. But they still bring with them the option of how to respond and whether that choice will move toward further stress or an easing of it. These occurrences might be as ordinary as an unexpected change in the weather that defeats the possibility of a planned get-together or a forgotten deadline landing on top of an already too tall list of to do items. It could be more severe, like a phone call with heartbreaking news or information that further complicates an already tenuous family issue.

How I respond comes from the question I asked my tearful friend: When I go to the deep part of myself, what will bring peace? If I choose to fight and push to have my way, no matter what, if I refuse to accept the facts of what is unchangeable, I will squander my inner equilibrium. On the other hand, if I can release the effort to have my expectations met and cease insisting everything be as I want, then tranquility makes a home in me.

Through the years when choices have needed to be made, I have learned how to respond based on both Christian and Buddhist teachings. Buddhism refers to one of the processes of arriving at peacefulness as *upekkha*, a Pali word meaning "equanimity." Gil Fronsdal from the Insight Meditation Center in Redwood, California, describes equanimity as the quality "that arises from the power of observation, the ability to see without being caught by what we see. When well-developed, such power gives rise to a great sense of peace. *Upekkha* can also refer to the ease that comes from seeing a bigger picture. Equanimity . . . is the ground for wisdom and freedom and the protector of compassion and love. While some may think of equanimity as dry neutrality or cool aloofness, mature equanimity produces a radiance and warmth of being."

When Sharon Salzberg writes about *upekkha*, she presents equanimity as having "balance" and then assures the reader that this does not mean having things such as our time and leisure be equally measured. "Instead," Salzberg explains, "it has to do with having perspective on life, and the effort you're putting out, and the changes you're going through. We establish this sense of balance within. It demands of us wisdom, and it gives us a growing sense of peace."

Episcopal priest Cynthia Bourgeault encourages the action of "surrender" as a part of spiritual growth. She describes it this way: "The word *surrender* itself means 'to hand oneself over' or 'entrust oneself.' It is not about outer capitulation but about inner opening. It is always voluntary, and rather than an act of weakness, it is always an act of strength." This strength is what I witnessed when my friend handed herself over to death and entrusted herself into God's care.

Through the years I've collected a file of Christian prayers of surrender. They are actually prayers of equanimity, expressing a willingness to yield, to give over to God what is happening. This willingness to yield is not a passive response, not "Oh well, just give up." Rather, this release involves a deliberate decision, a choice to enter into what is taking place and to cease the frantic striving to have things go a certain way. This surrender is one of assurance, in the words of the mystic Julian of Norwich that "all shall be well" no matter what happens.

United Methodist founder John Wesley echoes this surrender and acceptance when he prays: "I am no longer my own, but yours. Put me to what you will, rank me with whom you will; put me to doing, put me to suffering; let me be employed for you or laid aside for you, exalted for you or brought low for you; let me be full, let me be empty; let me have all things, let me have nothing. I freely and heartily yield all things to your pleasure and disposal."

The quip from *The Best Exotic Marigold Hotel* sort of sums up my approach to equanimity: "Everything will be alright in the end. If things are not alright, then it's not yet the end." How much easier and peacefully life proceeds when I trust that in the end, yes, everything will be alright, even if it is not what I desired. In the meantime, I have choices to make.

Elderhood Sunflower Prayer

Companion on my path of life, I turn to you with wonder and grati-tude. The season of the sunflower reminds me of what has unfolded in the seasons of my life.

Like sunflower seeds when they fall into readied soil prepared for their eventual growth,
I was sown in my mother's womb where your presence gestated in me.

Like sunflowers giving rise to a green stem that grows ever stronger in the summer,
I have observed my life unfold and gain strength through my root-edness in you.

Like sunflowers in bloom continually turning their bright yellow fac-es to the sunlight,
I have sensed your loving presence drawing me to you, Radiant Light of my soul.

Like sunflowers experiencing fierce thunderstorms of pelting rain and wild winds,
I have known unwanted storms of loss and have turned to you for strength.

Like sunflowers whose blooms gradually transform into abundant seeds of nurturance,
I trust that my virtues have produced a harvest, thanks to your abid-ing grace.

Like sunflowers whose blooms fade and physical appearance looks tattered,
I experience waning energy and bodily decline and turn to you to find my peace.

Gatherer of All,
like sunflowers whose life will be ended
when the combine comes to harvest them,
I will give my life over to you with trust
when you come for me in the hour of death.
All that my life has brought to fruition
will be left for future generations.
I bring what remains to be matured
and entrust this into your welcoming hands.
Thank you for faithfully guiding me
through the seasons of my life with you.
Amen.

September

This month leads us into Earth's harvest of plenty. The land's abundance epitomizes the effects of dedicated service. The harvest of the heart requires self-giving, attentive listening, and devoted love. We trust that kind deeds, however large or small, make a difference. We give generously of ourselves, trusting that the Holy One dwells within those we are serving.

Standing Beneath the Cross

When the final weeks
bowed to the journey of death

when time was just a blur

when muscles and bones
never felt so fatigued

and my mind dulled
into "just do it"

when tears captured
and stilled
every remnant of joy

when utter silence
arrived before dawn

and after the long vigil
finally ended—

gratefulness
to have been there,
with her, for her,
in devoted love
until the very last breath.

~ Joyce Rupp

Devoted Service

Serving from a place of effortless generosity we experience intimacy with all living things and we are naturally moved to care for those who are in pain.

~ **Gail Straub**

My brother-in-law's health gradually deteriorated after being diagnosed with Parkinson's disease. When I visited Jim and my sister, Lois, I discovered how devoted she was in tenderly giving herself to Jim's welfare. I also observed how my brother-in-law received her care. Affection, gratitude, and admiration for my sister shone in his eyes and reflected in his gentle smile. In the arduous situation of his increasing inability to care for himself, both of them had good reason to be impatient and disgruntled but neither of them gave in to these emotional responses. Instead, I witnessed a steady love nurtured over forty-five years of marriage.

Devotion and commitment are rooted strongly in the human heart, but it takes people whose love is large enough, strong enough, and generous enough to validate these essential gifts of an enduring relationship. This kind of love is learned and earned over a lifetime through a faithfulness purified in the fire of suffering. This quality of love precipitated Evelyn Underhill's questions to her readers in her book *The House of the Soul.* She based these invitations on the writing of St. John of the Cross: "Was everything that was done, done for love's sake? Were all the doors opened, that the warmth of Charity might fill the whole house; the windows cleaned, that they might more and more radiate from within its mysterious divine light?"

Love is meant to radiate from the doors and windows of our soul. When we witness this kind of dedication, it has the ability to change our hearts and influence our lives in the most unexpected ways. I am continually inspired and encouraged to live more unselfishly when I observe persons revealing this wide-hearted form of love.

Devoted service is not so much *what* we do but *how* we do it. Much depends on the intention motivating us toward service. My sister could easily have questioned, as Peter did with Jesus, "Look, we have left everything and followed you. What then will we have?" (Mt 19:27). She might have allowed herself to become swallowed in grudging self-pity and complaint. Instead, Lois stayed the course out of love, commitment, and compassion, giving herself to what was hers to do. Surely moments of impatience and irritation surfaced when she wished to be anywhere but where she was. After meeting these natural impulses, she set them aside. A dedicated, loving spirit prevailed.

At the same time, persons who give themselves totally in devoted service also need to care for themselves. If they fail to do this, they will tumble into all sorts of debilitating emotional traps. In *Standing at the Edge*, Joan Halifax describes this danger: "When we work too many hours, under untenable circumstances, for too little emotional reward—or when we feel our efforts aren't making a positive difference to others—these factors can push us to the limit of what we can sustain. From there, it's easy to fall over the edge and into the bleak landscape of burnout, where we feel jaded and demoralized."

Even so, there are those persons who make it through tough situations while being unable to provide little relief for themselves. Danuta Walesa, wife of Polish Solidarity trade union leader Lech Walesa, raised six children while he remained totally engaged in leading Poland from communism to democracy. Danuta was left alone much of the time. In spite of those difficult years when her anger welled up due to the isolation, she continued to be a devoted mother and supportive wife. Danuta did what she could to bring her best to an undesirable situation.

Even after death people can continue to inspire us by their devoted service. I learned this anew from my friend and coauthor Joyce Hutchison, who lived almost three years with stage-four lung cancer. A few months before her death, Joyce prepared her wake and funeral service. She voiced her intention to those of us present during the planning: "I want the theme to be about giving of ourselves. I hope this will be about love." Joyce explained how she approached her many years of oncology nursing and hospice work with the attitude of being a "foot washer." She shared how privileged she felt to be of service, having learned in nurses' training "to treat each patient as if that person were Jesus." Small wonder that Joyce's work revealed a tender heart filled with overflowing compassion.

Thus it came about that after Joyce's death, the evening wake service included the ritual of washing feet, based on the story of Jesus in John's gospel when he humbly washed the feet of his disciples (see Jn 13:1–17). This foot-washing made a profound statement about Joyce's approach to those who were a part of her work. It also encouraged those present to meet their relationships in a similar manner.

This foot-washing attitude is central to Caryll Houselander's message in *The Reed of God*: "We could scrub the floor for a tired friend, or dress a wound for a patient in a hospital, or set the table and wash up for the family; but we shall not do it in a martyr spirit or with that worse spirit of self-congratulation, of feeling that we are making ourselves more perfect, more unselfish, more positively kind. We shall do it for just one thing, that our hands make Christ's hands in our life, that our service may let Christ serve through us, that our patience may bring Christ's patience back to the world."

A life centered on this kind of love leads the way in devoted service.

Good Listeners

We were given two ears and one mouth for a reason, the philosopher Zeno observed. What you'll notice when you stop to listen can make all the difference in the world.

~ Ryan Holiday

While browsing through greeting cards, I came across one with this message: "Everyone needs a good listening to." Whoever came up with that one-liner knew a lot about human nature. In spite of how supportive a good listening to can be, fully attentive people are becoming an endangered species. In *Barking to the Choir,* Gregory Boyle offers a description of someone who definitely knew how to be an outstanding listener: "I consider it a singular blessing in my life to have known Cesar Chavez. Though many celebrate his vision, his community organizing skills, and his ability to create and galvanize a movement, I most remember and admire his keen skill at listening. If you were speaking to him, he wasn't looking over your shoulder, eyeing a more important person on the approach. Nothing and no one else existed in that moment but you and whatever you were going on about."

I found someone with that quality of listening after I returned from an enriching time in Peru. When I met Kathy for lunch she gave the gift of her genuine interest and complete attention to the details of my journey. I never once sensed she was bored or tired of my talking. I left the restaurant feeling grateful for her generosity. My friend allowed me to not only celebrate my joy but also expand it by the way her eager attentiveness took in my adventure.

Good listening is usually associated with attentiveness given for support and comfort when people speak about their troubles and misfortunes. Concentrated presence certainly does this by softening life's blows, but good listening also contributes to joy such as my friend gave me by her willingness to hear my stories. We provide added delight by our undivided attention, whether this be with a young child tugging at us to hear his playground story or an elder relating her prized memories.

In her poem "The Accolade," Marjorie Power received an affirmation for her ability to listen from a clerk in her neighborhood supermarket. As Power stood in line, the clerk told her that she had seen her picture in the newspaper. She then whispered to the poet that she had sensed "something special" about her "just from that listening you do, coming through the line."

Besides a one-to-one concentration of being fully present to an individual, good listening includes heeding what comes to us from the messages surfacing in our *internal* environment, the deeper realm of self where the Holy One whispers to us. In *Seven Thousand Ways to Listen,* Mark Nepo quotes Susan McHenry: "Deep listening is more than hearing with our ears, but taking in what is revealed in any given moment with our body, our being, our heart." These revelations often arrive in bits and pieces until they finally coincide and lead to new or revised guidance. This was the situation when I attended a stimulating conference in San Antonio, Texas. Soon after arriving at my hotel, I paused to read the complimentary newspaper. My heart leapt when I read an article about a new bicycle route—not because I'm a bicyclist, but because I'd been searching for a route in North America that could equal the soul-touching Spanish Camino I walked four years earlier.

The route traces one of the paths of the Underground Railroad and is now mapped from Mobile, Alabama, (a busy port for slavery) to Lake Huron Bay in Ontario (where slaves found freedom). This route has been established to "honor the bravery of those that fled from bondage and those that provided shelter." Upon reading about this I thought, *Maybe this is the American Camino I have been seeking.*

That evening at the opening of the conference, I was stunned by the first part of the program. Valerie Tutson presented a one-woman drama, a poignant and heart-rending account of a slave woman and her fear-filled, courageous flight to freedom. "That's it," said a voice inside of me, letting me know that what I heard onstage was connecting me with what I read earlier.

A year later, I left with Paula D'Arcy, a friend and writing colleague, to walk part of that Underground Railroad route in Alabama. Those two weeks turned out to be even more significant than anticipated. To this day, I value what came to me from attentive listening. The experience in Alabama taught me about the harrowing escape of slaves and their brave endurance of inhospitable conditions. Those days of walking where slavery had existed saturated my spirit with a desire to give my utmost to heal a world still caught in systemic racism.

When German mystic Hildegard of Bingen mourned the death of her treasured community member Rikkarda, she received comforting assurance by what she heard internally: "And then the crystalline voice emerges out of the landscape of articulated, moving parts. It is the Voice of Wisdom, she who has been with God from the beginning, from before the Fall, from beneath the Day Star. And her voice tells me that the time of mourning is past. . . . The Voice of Wisdom swells to bell-like resonance. It fills my head and beyond, to reverberate from the candlelit walls that enwomb me here. It is remarkable to see in this light how Rikkarda is loved by the Beloved."

Hildegard's experience indicates how deep listening can create a significant inner movement of the heart. Whether listening to another person, to our external or internal environment, good listening is as simple and as difficult as that.

A Temple Without Walls

... in each soul that may brush against my soul
God Who looks out at me.

~ Jessica Powers

While I was teaching at the Dromantine Center in Northern Ireland, Fr. Paddy loaned me his copy of *The Gentle Art of Blessing* by Pierre Pradervand. As Paddy handed the book to me, he commented, "I think you might like the contents." He was right. When I returned home, I purchased my own copy to savor the messages based on genuine reverence for everyone.

How we meet those we come in contact with makes all the difference. Pradervand writes, "To bless means to wish, unconditionally and from the deepest chambers of your heart, unrestricted good for others . . . to hallow, to hold in reverence, to behold with awe that which is always a gift from the Creator. . . . To bless is to acknowledge the omnipresent, universal beauty hidden from material eyes . . . When you wish them the very best from your innermost being, it is impossible for your heart not to expand. From a narrow cubicle, it will become a temple without walls."

A temple, cathedral, mosque, and any other site intended for worship, prayer, meditation, or sacred ceremony implies the possibility of connecting with a divine presence. What if we met one another with a similar expectation, with a faith-filled belief that divinity dwells here in this person? What if our hearts became temples without walls?

Some might consider this approach to be most difficult with strangers, but I admit to sometimes finding it more challenging to be a temple without walls for well-acquainted persons—relatives, colleagues, friends, and my religious community members. Maybe this is due to our becoming so familiar with these people that we simply forget the indwelling divine presence in them, whereas with strangers we might be inclined to be more deliberate. I relearned this several years ago when I had the privilege of leading a five-day retreat for my own Servite community. Almost all of our members were present. As I stood before them on the first day, I trusted in their acceptance of me. I did not feel a need to "prove myself" to them, nor they to me.

At the same time, I felt it would be valuable to remind each and all of us of our "temple quality." To do this, I began the retreat by inviting them to turn and face one other person. We then took turns asking the person facing us the question of 1 Corinthians 3:16: "Do you not know that you are God's temple, and that God's Spirit dwells in you?" Pausing to gaze quietly into the face of another sister or community associate and then asking that question allowed this beautiful reality to be imprinted on our hearts. This gesture reminded us to meet each one there with intentional reverence.

This notion of divinity dwelling within us first took root in my spiritual outlook when I was in my early twenties. I came across one of John Henry Newman's prayers and it had such drawing power that I decided to memorize the first part of it. I hoped that the intent of his prayer would gradually become true in my life. Since then, I have prayed my adapted version of his prayer every day—Newman addressed his prayer to Jesus; mine is to Holy Wisdom—no matter where I am or how I feel:

> Dear Sophia, thank you for dwelling within me and around me, for flooding my soul with your spirit and light. Penetrate and possess my whole being so utterly that all my life may be a radiance of yours. Shine through me and be so in me that everyone I come in contact with will feel your presence in my spirit. Let them look and see not just me, but you shining through me, and may I see you shining in them.

About five or six years ago I added that last piece—"and see you shining in them"—which is not in Newman's prayer. I wondered why I had not thought of that aspect sooner. Adding this dimension increased my awareness of the indwelling divine presence not only in myself but in everyone. These added words fortified my intention to be a temple without walls.

Many have been the occasions when this prayer has kept me from poisoning the waters of a valued relationship. Often have been the situations when this prayer changed my attitude and led me *toward* rather than away from someone whom I wanted to avoid. When I remember that my soul is flooded with the radiance of the Holy One's spirit and light, that I am to be a temple without walls, then my inner space expands in being a welcoming one.

This spaciousness occurred to me the day I hiked at a nature center in the wooded bluffs near Peoria, Illinois. Each of the trails included a special area with a bench and a wooden sign on which was carved the words "Listening Point." What impressed me the most about these listening places was the open, uncluttered landscape. Each area was set back off the trail about fifteen feet, in a spot with free space around the bench. This indicated both an invitation to come apart and listen and also a reminder to those who walked by to respect with silence the person sitting on the bench where he or she could listen to the deeper self within the inviting beauty of creation.

Living as a temple without walls does not, of course, exclude "boundary setting"—the necessity of protecting ourselves from people or situations that would allow harmful consequences if they entered our space. Limiting access to both our physical and interior selves can sometimes require this difficult decision. For the most part, however, the temple of our being is meant to be an openhearted presence.

As you consider what it is like to be a temple without barriers, you will find this most noticeable in your gestures of kindness, in the acceptance of diversity, in compassion for those who suffer, and in genuine respect for individuals whose lives do not mirror your own. Count yourself fortunate each time you are inspired to live as a temple without walls.

Small Seed, Big Harvest

A creative Life presses to birth within us.
It is a seed stirring to life if we do not choke it.
Here is the slumbering Christ, stirring to be awakened,
to become the soul we clothe in earthly form and
action.

~ Thomas R. Kelly

When I was a dinner guest at the home of my friends Mary and
Chuck, they invited me to go outside after the meal and look at
an unusual scene. The previous autumn they placed mulch around
the bushes next to their house. In summer a vigorous green plant
sprang up within the mulch. It grew, and grew, and grew. They had
no idea what it was as they watched the leaves expand daily. Then
the plant developed a thick stemmed vine that stretched extensively alongside the house. Large orange blossoms appeared about the
time my friends left for vacation. When they returned, they were
astonished to find the now-even-longer-vine held ten emerging but-
ternut squash. All this from a small seed hidden in a bag of mulch.

As I gazed in amazement at the plant's size and abundant produce, I marveled at the potential in one seed. On the way home, I
recalled an interview with Jane Goodall in the *Shambhala Sun* magazine. The famous primate researcher was asked what she saw as "the
most important thing individuals can do to affect positive change for
the environment." Goodall responded: "The most important thing
we can do is remember that every single day one of us makes a
difference." She went on to say, "The big problem today is that so
many people feel insignificant."

There seems to be a tendency in our society to think that the little things spoken or done are of slight notice or not as worthy compared to large gestures that make the news, such as copious philanthropy or outstanding altruism. With the exception of a brief blurb at the end of the national news or when a YouTube video goes viral, little merit is given to persons whose diminutive, ordinary words and actions result in having an exemplary influence on other people's lives.

Many of the redwood trees of the Pacific Northwest stand regally at 300 feet in height. They are prime examples of how something extremely tiny develops into something magnificent. A full-grown redwood tree will produce six to eight million seeds a year. These seeds are so teensy that a million of them weigh about eight pounds. What encouragement this gives me when I think of the smallness of my attempts to bring about something worthwhile.

Yesterday I held three tiny beefsteak tomato seeds in my hand. Our prayer facilitator led us in a meditation on what waits to germinate and grow within us. Mary read the reflection "Seed Song," which is in the May chapter of my book *Fresh Bread*. I rarely return to my books once they're published, so her reading of the seed's story awakened me anew to the amazing journey that a seed makes once it is placed in the soil.

That meditation brought me back to the Iowa countryside where I lived as a youth. Ever since those years I've been fascinated with the simplicity and the potential resting in a seed. My mind's eye can still see my father industriously planting acres and acres of corn. I knew that the small yellow kernel could spring up as tall, or taller, than an eight-foot stalk which would produce an ear of corn with more than six hundred kernels. All that from one single seed. Isn't that amazing?

The mysterious journey of spiritual growth is equally challenging and marvelous to behold. During retreats that I lead, I observe participants connecting with their own "seedness." Like my father planting kernels of corn, spiritual growth requires faith in our potential to reap a harvest. Then we take up the task of waiting like a seed in the darkness, trusting that the surrender is worth it. We open our whole being, ready to be drawn toward growth. We allow our roots of love to grow deep so they'll be sturdy and strong, so our spirituality will grow into fruition.

We may never know how a kernel of thoughtfulness and care stretches and grows, how some seemingly insignificant comment or action may well be that small seed in the mulch bag of life that ends up producing a surprising harvest. One word, one kind deed, one smile, one decision, one thank you, one phone call, one hug, one "I'm here for you," or one "I forgive you" can make a world of difference to another person. I know this to be true because I have both witnessed and experienced it.

As I look back, I see how one-seed-actions by dedicated and caring people influenced my life. A lot of those seeds were carried by people who never knew the impact they made. One question from my college professor altered the course for the rest of my life. ("Is that what you plan to do after you graduate?") One sympathy card eased the direction of grief over my father's death. (A shepherd's arms holding a lamb.) One line of a song revived my hope when discouragement was starving it. (From Leonard Cohen's "Anthem" song, about light getting through a crack.) One friend's positive statement led me forward. ("You have more strength within you than you know.")

Each day you and I hold within us seeds of all sorts of virtues. Whether or not those seeds germinate and grow depends mostly on us. Do we believe in this potential in us? Can we trust that no matter how insignificant our intentions and actions, they can make a positive difference in the life of another? Are the roots of our love ready to receive the divine energy that will assist with this growing process?

The next time you hesitate before lending a hand, writing a letter, risking a thoughtful comment, recycling an item, offering an affirmation, or giving an unsolicited donation, remember the small seed traveling in the bag of mulch. Think about a redwood tree rising high with incredible strength or a kernel of corn growing into hundreds more seeds to be sown, grown, and given for nourishment.

A Deep and Strong Trust

We trust the soul, its reality and power, its self-sufficiency, its capacity to speak truth, its ability to help us to listen and respond to what we hear.

~ **Parker Palmer**

In the devotional *Give Us This Day*, Alice Camille reflects on the oft-quoted passage from Ecclesiastes 3:1–11, "For everything there is a season": "Life is a pendulum, ceaselessly rocking. . . . Life can go either way—and in fact will go *both* ways, before it's over. Each of us will be happy and sad, strong and sick, winners and losers, before we're through. We'll celebrate and endure; know grand days and terrifying ones. We'll be glad to be alive. And wish we hadn't been born."

I was moving along in total agreement with Camille until that last line. It stopped me with a thud. I did a quick overview of my life. No, not even once have I ever regretted being born. My response has been the opposite: continual amazement and gratitude for being alive. Even though I have known low times, aching grief, and needling regrets, along with despondent episodes regarding both political and ecclesiastical duplicity, I have continually been glad to have been born.

While I approach life as absolutely precious, I also understand why someone might find this journey of existence too much and wish to not have been part of it. If I experienced a life of tragedy after tragedy, physical and sexual abuse, unyielding physical pain, incessant mental and emotional anguish, being stuck in dire poverty no matter how hard I worked, or moving in and out of the kind of depression Parker Palmer describes as "you're not *in* darkness, you *become* darkness," I could wish to not have been born.

I want to avoid being condescending, arrogant, or easily satisfied by my own experience and attitude toward being birthed. Besides the gift of being born, this reality instills in me a keener sense of compassion for those who suffer and a fuller resolve to do what I can to ease the burdens of those for whom life holds little optimism. How people facing extremely burdened situations go on with their lives does astound me.

When reading about the life of Mother Teresa of Calcutta, I was surprised to learn of the demanding challenges that confronted her long before she ever began the compassionate ministry of caring for impoverished ill and dying people. After teaching in India for seventeen years as a woman religious, Mother Teresa felt a powerful call to found a new community to care for the poorest of the poor. To do this, she had to request formal permission from the central Office for Religious Congregations in the Vatican, in whose hands her vision for the future rested. This entailed having to prove the validity of her personal and spiritual capabilities and to endure lengthy waits to receive responses to her letters. When the responses finally did arrive, there was often another question or concern from Rome yet to be answered. Nothing happened quickly. Mother Teresa continually submitted to the process, although at times she grew impatient with the slowness of it.

Mother Teresa had to trust what moved deeply within her, to believe in what she felt she ought to do, and at the same time, stay closely united with the One whom she believed had called her to make this radical change of direction. When Brian Kolodiejchuk, M.C., describes these excruciating years of Mother Teresa's, he points to what allowed her to not give up: "Yet her wealth lay in her heart: unshakable faith in God and absolute confidence in the promise He had made to her two years earlier: 'Do not fear—I shall be with you always . . . Trust me lovingly—trust me blindly.'"

I also learned a lot about trust from a woman I met ten years ago when I traveled to northern Minnesota to join a group of women for retreat on a peninsula only reachable by boat. There I pitched my tent for five days and relished the comfort of sighing pine trees, the haunting call of loons, and stars dangling like diamond orbs in the pitch-black night. But what gave me the greatest pleasure was the presence of a wise woman named Trish who led the retreat. I observed how she entered into life with unusual acceptance and openness in spite of the death of close friends, several accidents with serious bone breakages, plus hospitalizations for illness. Two years earlier her house burned down, destroying her computer and every book, article, poem, piece of music, and all her retreat resources.

In spite of this enormous loss, she had not allowed any of this to crush her spirit. Here was Trish, accepting life as it is, not as one longs for it to be. She was giving herself fully to the present moment, serving others by leading the retreat, and trusting that what was needed would be there for her. And it was. I learned a lot about acceptance, letting go, and moving on. One of her pithy quips that stayed with me was "Let go—or be dragged." That saying brought some laughter, but it also touched a common chord with those of us in the circle. We heard loud and clear the value of trust in order to live with serenity and to have the energy we need to be there for others.

In September where I live, Earth slowly turns us toward autumn. In several months we will be swallowed by winter's darkness. The trees and vegetation will once again be a witness to the endless cycle of regeneration, to the necessity of low times, gray days, and muted activity—so unlike the high-spirited movement of summer. The autumn and winter seasons will speak to being patient, to trust that some sort of growth or new life follows hard times and seemingly hopeless situations.

Life is full of undulation, tumbling, stretching, falling down, and getting up. I recognize how I must give myself over with trust when life is going well and not going so well. In all of this, one thing is sure, I am happy that I was born.

A Prayer for Caregivers

Compassionate Caregiver, many who rise on this day
will spend exhausting hours providing care for others.
They will do this because of a dedication grounded on love
or by the requirements of duty—or maybe both.

They will exert their energy, become weary in spirit and body
through their unstinting kindness and unpretentious love.
They will tend unceasing details to ensure others' wellbeing.
When the day concludes and their exiled verve is depleted,
who will be the attentive, kindhearted caregiver for them?

Wrap your compassionate cloak around these tired ones.
Strengthen and revitalize their exhausted bodies and spirits.
Urge caregivers to be gracious to their worn-out selves.
Convince them that they are worthy of being kindly tended.

Restore their fatigue with your shepherding presence
as it is lived and shared through other human beings,
those who understand the challenge of continually giving.
May these compassionate and thoughtful persons
be the expression of your inner refreshment
for those who are giving their best to care for others.

~ Joyce Rupp

October

The falling leaves and empty grain fields of autumn reflect a similar emptiness that can take place in the human spirit. When caught in the throes of unwanted afflictions, we draw from our courage, persistence, and resiliency. Amid these challenging transitions and fierce difficulties, we relinquish what we must and receive strength from our Refuge and Shelter.

Yielding

Prairie grass sways elegantly, dances
on a hillside covered with wild flowers;
supple and unencumbered six-foot stems
bend and yield to murmuring breezes.

Later that day, I am in a screened-in porch,
eye-level with a spacious sycamore tree;
I sit there reading until an insistent rustle
begs loudly for my undivided attention.

I look to see autumn leaves, like prairie grass,
yielding without the least hesitation,
giving themselves to the breathy gusts,
shimmering, shaking, completely at ease.

Silence returns. Except for the little cheeps
of a nearby bird contentedly lullabied
with the droning of sleepy insects
given over to summer's leftover heat.

I begin to chide myself for failing to assume
a similar, unfettered freedom. But then
gratitude arises for the desire to give myself
that fully, to want to yield with complete trust
to the breath of Spirit, to the grace-filled Wind.

~ Joyce Rupp

Relinquishment

Toward the end, while it was difficult for her to relinquish a life full of activity and expectation and to accept that her future was limited, she found something of value in each day.

~ Ira Brock

The sight of a palo verde tree filled with dried seedpods caused me to pause when I walked near Spirit in the Desert Retreat Center in Carefree, Arizona. I felt compelled to stand before the tree to contemplate it for a while. The seedpods were within my reach, so I stretched my hand upward and took several from the branch. As I examined them, I noticed how they bore a resemblance to peapods. But what actually seized my attention was how almost every pod had burst open and flung its seeds forth in a hope-filled gesture of fecundity.

Those empty pods triggered a memory of an afternoon walk several weeks earlier when I came upon a clump of daylilies by a sidewalk. Their flowers, too, had been transformed into small seedpods. When I touched a daylily pod, it sprang open like a miniature cannon. Tiny, round, black seeds bounded out quicker than my eye could follow as they leapt through the air and down to the ground. I smiled at their eagerness to give themselves away.

I am not sure how long I lingered beneath the palo verde tree. My feet didn't want to move because my mind and heart were ardently taking in lessons about spiritual development. The sight of those emptied seed pods urged me to be more passionate and enthusiastic about the kind of relinquishment that led the palo verde to release what it diligently engaged in during the intense summer heat of the Sonoran Desert.

Each year the autumn trees in Iowa speak to me about a similar abdication. They tell me about the impermanence of life and to not cling to what I hold held dear when it's time for letting go. While I relish autumn's quiet way of gradually slowing down the activity in nature, at the same time, I resist what it tells me. Mainly because it pokes death in my face everywhere I turn.

I don't like the inherent quality of impermanence within this season. I don't want to let go of summer's warmth and energizing green. I yearn to hold on tightly to the spacious days of light and easy access to outdoor activity. I take a long, loving look at summer, trying to convince my heart to not grasp tightly, to be grateful for what I treasured about the season and then let it be. Even so, no matter how old I get or how many encouraging lessons come my way about the cyclical necessity of fullness and emptiness, detachment remains somewhat of a snag for me.

Fortunately, my resistance eases by observing the way other people respond to the relinquishment process. Last week a participant at a retreat described how she bid farewell to her ninety-eight-year–old father. The two of them shared a profound love for one another. As her father lay dying, he whispered to her, "I tried to stay here for you as long as I could." The beloved daughter held him tenderly and uttered these releasing words, "Dad, it's okay for you to go and join Mom." And with that, he departed. What immense love in that final relinquishment.

One of the helpful explanations I've read regarding this process of attaching and then detaching comes from Angeles Arrien in *The Four-Fold Way*. Arrien encourages investing oneself fully in life while being "open to outcome, not attached to outcome." She goes on to explain, "Most Westerners equate the word *detachment* with 'not caring.' Linguistically, however, *detachment* is most often defined as 'the capacity to care deeply from an objective place.'"

Someone who exemplified an ability to fully invest herself and yet not be attached to the outcome is Etty Hillesum, a Jewish Dutch woman who died at age twenty-nine during World War II. Three months before she boarded a Nazi train taking her to the gas chambers at Auschwitz, Etty sensed that death was closing in on her and wrote the following in her journal:

> Living and dying, sorrow and joy, the blisters on my feet and the jasmine behind the house, the persecution, the unspeakable horrors—it is all as one in me, and I accept it all as one mighty whole and begin to grasp it better if only for myself, without being able to explain to anyone else how it all hangs together. I wish I could live for a long time so that one day I may know how to explain it, and if am not granted that wish, well, then somebody else will perhaps do it, carry on from where my life has been cut short. And that is why I must try to live a good and faithful life to my last breath, so that those who come after me do not have to start all over again, do not face the same difficulties.

Etty's reflection reveals a great amount of strength and wisdom by giving herself intently to life, while also being ready to release this desire completely if that meant the final outcome for her. Etty's astonishing surrender confirms what Robert Wicks states in *Crossing the Desert*: "If the call to let go of the old and the familiar is responded to when the time is ripe then incredible freedom and love are possible."

So it is that each autumn I face the big questions: how to cherish who and what I have and how to hold these gifts freely without clinging so strongly to them that the possibility of my growth is suffocated. I think I am getting better at relinquishment, but I still sense a certain reluctance. This October I am seeking inspiration from the dying leaves gathering in ever deeper layers on the lawn. I see the trees letting go of what enabled them to sip the nourishing rays of summer sun. The leaves they relinquish will eventually become a rich humus to nourish spring's greening growth.

Maybe, just maybe, this will be the year when I truly welcome that process in myself.

Strength of My Soul

God is our refuge and strength,
a very present help in trouble.

~ Psalm 46:1

One morning when I sleepily began praying with Psalm 138, the third verse woke me up: "You increased the strength of my soul." *How*, I wondered, *could my soul need strength, and what kind of strength might that be?* I set aside this question after a quick answer did not arrive. But in the following week, lo, there it was again and again, that word *strength*. It showed up constantly in the Psalms. Here are a few of them:

"O my strength, I will watch for you" (59:9).
"You will strengthen their heart" (10:17).
"Sing aloud to God our strength" (81:1).
"The LORD is my strength and my shield" (28:7).
"I love you, O LORD, my strength" (18:1).
"Happy are those whose strength is in you" (Psalm 84:5).

Now when this sort of unexpected connection happens, I wake up. What was the Spirit trying to tell me? I was ready to delve into the meaning of the phrase "strength of my soul." I pondered the words "spiritual strength" and decided this was like a spiritual muscle, one that held potency of purpose, tenacious courage, power beneath seeming weakness, bravery to hold on, durable perseverance, willingness to stand firmly in spite of seeming defeat, and fortitude amid the forces of impossibility.

How could my soul, the firm core of my being, require that powerful kind of reinforcement? Wasn't *soul* a fundamental part of a human being, unchanging and undaunted by whatever charged against it? Could *soul* be weak and vulnerable? After looking at how I encounter life emotionally and mentally, I realized that yes, each day all sorts of things can assail this pure core, trying to lessen her effectiveness as an all-prevailing reservoir of love.

After some reflection, I could easily name a number of interior experiences I've counted on for my soul to have strength to face: when doubt proposes that small gestures of compassion do not make a difference; when kindness struggles to stay alive while anger sinks its teeth into negative rhetoric with the urge to repeat the same irate stuff; when the pressure of work tries to persuade me to not use time for prayer; when I vacillate about the decision to step away from personal concerns and be a caring presence for someone who's hurting; and when I forget to live with daily gratitude for all sorts of gifts that are distractedly passed over.

A few weeks after recognizing that my soul certainly needs strength, I came across something amazing to reinforce my understanding of this. As I drove to the post office, I looked out the window and couldn't believe what I saw beside me—a glistening spider web attached from the side mirror to the top of the car door's upper frame. At the middle of this web, a teeny spider no bigger than a pencil eraser clung with amazing tenacity to the center of the thin filaments. At each stop light I looked again to gain assurance of its presence. I could only view the web when the sunlight angled just right, so I kept observing closely. As I did, I became aware of drivers next to me at the stoplights who might be thinking I was a bit insane as I fixed my eyes on seemingly nothing at all. Nevertheless, I studied that little spider intently, in awe that its home could endure the force of the wind created by the car's speed.

During the following days, each time before I entered the car I checked to see if the spider managed to keep his life and home intact. Sure enough, he stayed safely in place. The more I befriended this tiny companion, the more I thought about the profound metaphor his delicate yet durable web offered regarding soul-strength. In the previous essay, "Relinquishment," I emphasized what most teachers of inner growth insist on: letting go as being indispensable for greater wholeness. That appraisal contains substantial truth. However, holding on and remaining firm are equally vital for maintaining integrity and inner durability. There is a time for clinging, for holding fast.

As the spider could not survive without the web's tough filaments, I cannot survive without a steadfast relationship with the spiritual filament of my life. My soul requires this reliable and enduring quality. Jessica Powers' poem "The Garments of God," refers to this need to hold on firmly: "God sits on a chair of darkness in my soul . . . here in the dark I clutch the garments of God." Clutching and holding steadfastly like that tiny spider on the strong web—there are times on our spiritual journey when this is about all we can manage to do.

When I adhere to this divine presence, I find encouragement and inspiration to live my best. I've known the value of attaching my deepest self to this Beloved One: while living in the bleakness of long-lasting grief; when yearning for world peace and seeing instead the world violently torn apart; in making decisions to work through conflicts instead of running from them; in choosing to live simply in spite of the long arm of greedy consumerism trying to break my hold; and by maintaining long-lasting relationships, even when these sometimes prove disappointing.

One other lesson I observed from the spider's resilient web involves its flexibility. I noticed the web endured because it gave itself to the wind's movement rather than remaining rigid. I saw how the web billowed in and out according to the velocity of travel. So here I am again, coming full circle to surrender.

When to hang on tightly, and when to let go freely? This question remains a continuous paradox. The spider withstood what threatened to overcome it. So will I—if my inner web can be both sturdy and supple.

Sipping from Mud Puddles

Resilience is built into the very cells
of our bodies. It is as much a part of us
as our ability to heal.

~ Resmaa Menakem

Messages come to me from people I have never met, describing situations that have beaten them down. I recently received this kind of letter from a frazzled woman whose father has dementia, her husband suffers from ongoing depression, and several of her young children have learning disabilities. All this, while she tries to work full-time. No wonder this person's life feels heavily burdened. Little surprise that she feels overwhelmed and questions the reason or purpose for what is taking place. She is far from alone in bearing way too many afflictions.

Through the ages, humans have struggled with insurmountable obstacles and what to do about them. In the book of Judges (6:11–24), Gideon wildly threshes wheat in a wine press, hurrying to finish and hide the grain before his enemies get access to it. He's obviously grouchy about having to do this. When an angel appears and announces that God is with him and he is to go and deliver his people from Midianites, the first words from Gideon's mouth slip out disgruntledly: "If the LORD is with us, why then has all this happened to us?" Gideon doesn't stop there. He challenges the angel: "And where are all [God's] wonderous deeds that our ancestors recounted to us?" No answer is given. Instead, Gideon is told, "Go in this might of yours. . . ." In other words, go with the inner strength you have. Gideon objects and says his family is the weakest clan and that he is "the least" in his family. But Gideon eventually goes on as he is told. He relies on his soul's resilience and the One who sends him forth. In doing so, Gideon completes successfully the task assigned to him.

Like Gideon, and anyone facing unwanted circumstances, sometimes that's all we can do—just go on with whatever strength we have—even if it's meager—and trust in better days to come. If only we could take to heart and accept the self-confidence that psychotherapist Patrick Fleming offers: "Soul resilience is based in the felt knowledge of a deep part of us that we call soul, which always remains whole, untouched, alive and seeking a pathway to healing and life. It is the unconsciousness that at our core there is a wellspring of energy, hope and purpose, that ultimately cannot be shattered, even by the worst of traumas. We all possess this inner spiritual resilience, this lifespring of the soul that we can tap to carry us through and beyond our personal traumas and trials and those occurring in our society."

I thought of *soul resilience* when I went for my daily walk after a heavy rain shower. A bright red cardinal sipping from a mud puddle in the middle of the path caught my attention. As I watched the bird's quiet, easy way of drinking, I wondered about the taste of that cloudy water. I didn't notice any distasteful grimaces from the bird. The cardinal seemed quite satisfied and kept on sipping. The griminess in that puddle reminded me of what life resembles during troublesome periods. We have to be satisfied with a lack of clarity in our mud-puddle stage, to find what can nourish and sustain us until better days. Maybe brief glimmers of hope, a message of reassurance, or a voice of empathy provide the only sustenance available when we are deeply troubled or overwhelmed with what feels like way too much to handle.

Being with people who know how to sip from mud puddles often restores my belief and trust in soul resilience. A few years ago, I gave a three-day retreat in Montana. I have only spoken in that beautiful state on three occasions, but each time I've been in awe of the people I've met. Montanans have an incredible inner strength, an ability to endure. Their big sky country is sparsely populated, and the residents drive amazingly long distances for events that bring them together. They endure the harshness of the winters but also thrive on the natural beauty of the land.

As I listened to their personal experiences, I kept noticing how resilient the participants were. This started the first night with a woman telling me her only child had died a month earlier. I stood amazed that she had the emotional strength to come to the retreat. She explained how her ability to endure her grief was affirmed after discovering my poem about the resiliency of an evergreen tree as a metaphor for human resiliency. After that conversation, it seemed that an awareness of soul hardiness leapt out from everywhere. The dearest of all was a tall, pencil-thin woman named Peggy. Her badly bruised arms revealed treatments for a recurrence of cancer. She wore a jaunty blue hat to cover her just-beginning-to-grow-out hair. Peggy exuded a radiant joy throughout the days, seemingly undaunted by her lack of physical stamina.

We tend to forget that we have within us a mighty reservoir of strength. And how good it is to be among those who witness the human spirit's ability to survive all sorts of hardship and distress. I doubt these resilient people realize the gift they give to the rest of us when they stand strong in their struggles and unknowingly demonstrate how they are managing to withstand what confronts them.

A friend of mine working as a pastoral minister described how she encouraged soul resiliency when addressing a group of hurting folks. Ginny chose to read Romans 8:35–39, which begins: "What will separate us from the love of Christ? Will anguish, or distress, or persecution, or famine, or nakedness, or peril, or sword?" She then asked those present to reflect on what they thought might be attempting to separate them from their inner resiliency. She gave a few examples: serious illness, constant loss, unwanted transitions, fear of failure, aging's limitations, and financial insecurity.

After hearing about that, I asked myself: *What keeps me from inner peace and a lack of trust in divine support during my mud-puddle times?* A lot of options tumbled through my mind: big and little irritations, death of friends, inconveniences and disappointments, troubling and sorrowful news, the reality of racism, and other damaging systems. And then came the questions: *Would I allow any of this to keep me from being a considerate and caring person? Would any of this have the power to separate me from my Teacher of Compassion?*

What about you? Would anything separate you from the love of Christ during your mud-puddle experiences?

You Can Do This Hard Thing

Those endure who seek to do what is deeply important
to them, no matter how difficult it may be.

~ Joan Chittister

While on retreat, I learned a lot from sitting in front of an aged
maple tree with broad branches. One leaf in particular caught my
attention as it swayed in the breeze. I was taken with the leaf, not
because it was hanging directly in front of me but because one third
of its forest-green self had disappeared. Nothing there. Just empty space, as if someone performed a surgical amputation. I do not
know whether a voracious insect ate that part or if the wind ripped
it away. What I do know is that the rest of the leaf remained alive
and thriving.

That leaf became a metaphor regarding pieces of my life that
felt ragged and torn by unwanted events, yet not all had been destroyed. I marveled at how much remained positive and prosperous
in spite of the empty patches. I recalled Carrie Newcomer's song,
"You Can Do This Hard Thing." The verses of the song describe
instances of something she either felt she could not do or did not
want to do. During these challenging situations she was encouraged
to continue onward because someone believed she could do what
was difficult, even though following through with it would not be an
easy thing to do.

Every man and woman who deliberately went into the ravages
caused by the September 11 terrorist attack moved forward with
courage, trusting they could do the tough things of rescuing, sorting
through the ashes and rubble, counseling the distraught, and tending
the injured. Healthcare workers during the COVID-19 pandemic

had to call on their deepest reserves of strength and compassion while they watched so many patients dying without loved ones by their side. Brave persons joined in the Black Lives Matter protests and risked doing the challenging and dangerous act of drawing attention to systemic racism.

Some circumstances we can't avoid. We have to trust in our ability to meet them head-on, to have our courage coaxed forth so we can make it through to the other side. Think back on your life's disturbing times, how you managed to get though what upset and almost bowled you over. These memories can help us retain our ability to not cave in to dreaded experiences when they force their way into our lives and threaten to destroy every remnant of peace in us.

I relearnt this from my friend Dorothy when she lay dying of ALS disease and could barely speak. She turned to me in her pain and whispered, "I'm so tired of being blind and sick. I wish I would not linger long." She then recalled a memory that seemed to strengthen her resolve to bear what she knew she could not change. I strained to hear Dorothy's words as she spoke of her mother, a loving woman always feeding people who were poor. At the end, her mother had also been blind and died with agonizing pain. Dorothy found strength from something her mother said in response to a question Dorothy asked her: "How can you stand it?" Her unshakable mother said simply, "You endure what you must endure." Like her mother, Dorothy *did* endure and died peacefully a few days later.

Black Elk, the far-seeing Lakota medicine man of faith, also knew how to do the hard things life demanded of him. In *Blessed Among Us*, Robert Ellsberg describes how Black Elk, when just nine years old, received a powerful vision calling him to help his people. Black Elk gave himself generously to this vision but eighteen years later this commitment shattered when the U.S. army killed more than three hundred of his Lakota tribe in the massacre of Wounded Knee. With his vision torn to shreds, Black Elk felt devastated, but he did not buckle under the pain, nor did he give in to cynicism or revenge. Instead, he gradually moved forward to be of service in another way. Twelve years after marrying a Catholic woman,

Black Elk joined her church, blended parts of his Lakota spirituality with hers and became a catechist, traveling extensively to share the Church's teachings.

Many are the courageous people who dedicated their lives to a vision or purpose that fell apart in their lifetimes. What can we learn from them? What inspiration might we draw from their efforts and their response? One insight especially stands out: the human spirit houses an amazing capacity that enables people to rise up after harsh experiences knock them down. In spite of the utter failure of his vision, Black Elk found a loving companion, a faith that sustained him, and a meaningful way to share this gift. It wasn't anything like he envisioned, but he had the bigness of heart to be led in another direction.

A part of our lives may appear to be lost like that maple leaf, like the end of Black Elk's hope for his Lakota tribe, but the innate hope stored in the human spirit endures. Black Elk's heart grew larger. His compassion expanded. When a part of our lives, our dreams, and our hopes, has been taken from us, we turn toward what grounds us and prevents our hope from eroding. We look to what enables us to retain our spiritual bearings until we can manage to accept what has been lost, until we can turn the corner toward what lies ahead and regain our passion for life.

There's a passage in St. Paul's second letter to the Corinthians that offers support for those who feel pressed upon and laid low when strife invades and dominates their life. Paul assures the people that they (and us) are like clay jars holding the treasure of divinity and that this "extraordinary power" provides a mainstay in times of trouble: "We are afflicted in every way, but not crushed; perplexed, but not driven to despair; persecuted, but not forsaken; struck down, but not destroyed" (2 Cor 4:7–9).

Knowing we have this ability to endure, we assure ourselves and those around us, "You can do this hard thing. You can be that partially destroyed leaf and still go on to be alive and thriving. You have it within you to do so."

Don't Give Up

We want to dare greatly. We all want to be brave.

~ **Brené Brown**

After a colleague described how distressed she felt about the hatred and violence filling the daily news, she sighed, "I am about ready to give up on humanity." My heart plummeted on hearing that conclusion. After my initial protest of "Oh no, you can't give up," I then acknowledged she had good cause to feel that way. Were I to name the problems on our planet, the list could extend indefinitely. Even so, I assured her I could also name many reasons for keeping hope close to our hearts.

Webster's Unabridged Dictionary defines hope as "a desire for some good, accompanied with at least a slight expectation of obtaining it, or a belief that it is obtainable. Confidence in a future event. Trust. Reliance." Joan Halifax refers to hope as "one that allows us to see a different future. John Paul (Lederach) has called this *the creative imagination*, the ability to envision the future in a way that rehumanizes all the players and creates the possibility for transformative change, even against all odds. This species of imagination points to resilient purpose and revolutionary patience, the capacity to be not afraid or impatient as we imagine a vaster horizon than we had believed possible."

This certainly defines the lives of Carrie Chapman Catt, Elizabeth Cady Stanton, Millicent Garrett Fawcett, and other valiant women who gave their all for obtaining the right to vote. In spite of the debilitating defamation of their character along with imprisonment by the threatened opposition, these women let their hearts stay firmly fixed on what was possible. They *did* dare greatly. They *were* brave and did not give up. Trust in their ability to bring about change kept them dreaming of what could be, ought to be, and must be. And one day women *did* win the right to vote, thanks to these tenacious justice-seekers.

Believing change can happen requires a persistent amount of not giving up. Last year while at the lovely mountains of North Carolina, I walked over to the conference building where I was scheduled to speak. I noticed a maintenance man swishing a large broom in the air near the entry way. As I greeted him, he turned around and sputtered, "These pesky spider webs. I can't get rid of them. One day I sweep them down and the next day they're back again." The rest of the day I thought about those spiders, about their "peskiness" to keep weaving their webs in the face of what seemed like daunting defeat.

Persistence as enduring as those spiders leads me to ask, *Do I have that kind of limitless determination in my own small efforts to lessen the suffering of those close to me and those far away? Can I trust my compassionate care and actions to help heal our world?* I hope for this, but I will have to be as unwavering as the spiders, as faith-filled as people working for justice, to not give up when my tiny efforts seem ineffective or when the vastness of the world's pain appears too enormous for me to touch.

Spiders know instinctively to keep at it and not give up. Humans have this inherent ability, too, but when obstacles continually descend like large brooms sweeping away hard-attained goals, they can forget they have a persistent nature that makes it possible to keep on keeping on.

The urge to not give up became embedded in me as a child. Every spring my father worked long, hard days on our family farm, planting oat and corn seeds in our fields. I watched his enduring faith and courage as he trusted his efforts would be worth it. Even at a young age, I realized how much conviction it took to do that planting. A cornfield could develop and look glorious as it filled with tall, deep green stalks. But the leaves might be stripped and the crop severely damaged with just one quick-passing hailstorm. Or the field of oats could do well throughout the summer but right before ripening enough to be harvested, a fierce windstorm could flatten the stems to the ground and wipe out the possibility of gathering the grain.

The biblical story of Noah in the book of Genesis (8:6–12) contains a potent metaphor regarding standing strong for a better future when difficulties overwhelm and try to drown that possibility. After a long sojourn on the flooded seas, Noah sent a dove out from the ark, "to see if the waters had subsided from the face of the ground; but the dove found no place to set its foot, and it returned to him in the ark, for the waters were still on the face of the whole" (Gn 8:8–9). Instead of giving up, Noah waited. He did not stop believing. He sent out the dove again. Still no sign of land. He continued to be convinced they would find it.

Noah persisted for another week, and once more sent out the dove. This time, the dove returned with a tiny sign of life: an olive leaf in its beak. It took yet one more extended waiting period before Noah sent the dove out. This time the bird did not return—and so this story became one of hope for every person whose life takes them far from the land of security and into the sea of uncertainty.

When we face obstacles that block the path to our desire for change, when we yearn for a better future, it is time to not give up. Rather, it is a call to believe in what is not yet visible. We send out the dove of persistence through our prayer and in our faith that the One much wiser than us will lead and guide us. We give ourselves to trust, like Noah, that what we hope for will eventually appear on the horizon. We keep sending out the dove.

A Prayer of Anchoring

We who have taken refuge might be strongly
encouraged to seize the hope set before us.
We have this hope, a sure and steadfast anchor of the soul,
a hope that enters the inner shrine behind the curtain.

~ Hebrews 6:18–19

Holy One, how quickly my inner world can be thrown off balance. Without a strong anchor in your abiding presence, I am carried along like an untethered boat in the swift current of life. My relationship with you serves to keep steady my internal boat. This anchoring lessens an urge to be engulfed in the tidal waves of distress and the deluge of activity. I turn to you and pray:

Anchor my worries in your unswerving serenity
residing beneath the turbulent waves in myself.

Anchor longings and action for world peace
in the steady stream of your insistent justice.

Anchor a respect for every human being
in the clear waters of your nonjudgment.

Anchor deeply in your merciful forgiveness
any urges I have toward retaliation.

Anchor my talents in generous service and
energize them in the currents of your grace.

Anchor in the depths of your divine wisdom
questions and concerns about an uncertain future.

Anchor unavoidable turmoil that riles my spirit
in the gracious tranquility of your abiding love.

Anchor every heartbeat and breath of mine
in the expansive ocean of your compassion.

185

November

Within this mellow passageway from summer's source of plenty to the arrival of winter's barrenness, baskets of restorative memories spill over into gratitude. The soul thrives by recalling those persons who generated a positive influence on our lives. The joy of kinship with both the living and the dead is celebrated. Forgotten gifts regain a fresh appreciation.

The Power of Fragrance

At the farmers' market I browse booths
overflowing with local garden wealth.
In a moment of surprise I am drawn
like moth to a candle. The familiar fragrance
lingering from past days on the farm:
dill in Mom's garden. Tall, shaggy plants
with their skinny stems, lacy-seeded tops,
looking more like flowers than herbs.

Memories pour forth, as a youth
standing by my hard-working mother,
sweating as we work together by the old stove
in the dimly-lit basement, filling quart jars
with pickles and tufts of dill on the top.
More memories rush in: early mornings
in the garden, weeding, hoeing, bending low,
swatting off determined insects, kneeling
until the creases wore lines of dried mud
while I picked buckets of matured vegetables.

I muse as I walk away from the farmer's booth,
a big bunch of dill clutched loosely in my hand:
how I enjoyed that drudgery in the garden,
why it seemed more pleasure than pain,
more joy than a grudging duty to be done.
Perhaps it was the generous fragrance
of dill wafting across the spacious garden
that kept my spirit so decidedly happy.

~ Joyce Rupp

Sustaining Positive Memories

I am convinced that our joyful memories have often
been overlooked, like some undiscovered gold.

~ Macrina Wiederkehr

Among his teachings found *In Search of Being,* philosopher G. I.
Gurdjieff describes memory as "a very imperfect device by which
we make use of only a small part of our store of impressions. But
once experienced, impressions never disappear; they are preserved
on the discs where they are recorded." Scientific researchers have
found that one way these impressions are stored is through scent.
My niece Chris experienced this when she inherited my mother's
sewing box. As Chris opened the box, she caught the fragrance of
Mom's favorite perfume and exclaimed, "Grandma!" This was followed by sharing stories of the woman she loved.

The German mystic Hildegard of Bingen referred to the power
of scent when she accessed a valued memory that drew her inward.
In a journal entry she describes herself as a young child, gathering
some of the first plants of spring. She found these in places that were
"low, hidden, pungent, and musky smelling." Hildegard brought
the leaves, petals, and blossoms home to put beneath her quilt. She
remembers, "Some of the smells always remained . . . it was like
sleeping in a fragrant meadow; after a while I could even carry the
secret fragrance with me into the clear light of day. More and more
I learned to coax myself into the inner world."

Remembrances associated with a positive scent keep us in touch
with the pleasures we've known. They can also reconnect us to our
loved ones, along with helping to balance discontent when it swirls
through us. We can retain hope's aliveness with positive memories

when we pause to deliberately recall who and what gifted us by holding us in the arms of kindly acceptance. This, in turn, affects our emotional tone.

Memories also hold the potential for internal change. Linda Hogan alludes to this possibility in *The Woman Who Watches Over the World:* "'Memory is a field full of psychological ruins,' wrote French philosopher Gaston Bachelard. For some that may be true, but memory is also a field of healing that has the capacity to restore the world, not only for the one person who recollects, but for cultures as well. When a person says 'I remember,' all things are possible."

In accessing a memory, Macrina Wiederkehr suggests these ways: "First of all, you have to acknowledge its presence in your life. Secondly, you will need to spend a lot of time with your soul. The soul thrives on remembering. Feed it memories and it comes alive."

I discovered this to be true one morning when I was grousing about the nasty weather as I walked into our prayer group. We already had a lot of snow and the air was again filling with the white stuff. I struggled to drive across the city on streets still icy from freezing rain a few days before. As far as I was concerned, winter had become a royal pain in the you-know-what. To my surprise, our leader that day invited us to look out the window at the beauty of the gently falling snow. She commented on the splendor of the large, intricately designed snowflakes that landed on her car's cold windshield that morning.

Wow, I thought. *Guess it's time for a little attitude change.* Then, Kathi encouraged us to spend our time of silent prayer by reflecting on a positive memory of winter. As soon as I went deeper into the silence, I entered into a lovely, sensual scene of my childhood winters on the farm. I could visualize and smell the delicious fried dough-bread covered with sugar that my mother made on snowy days. I saw her handing some to me to take to my father out in his farm shop. There I found the aroma of wood burning in the old pot-bellied stove that kept Dad warm while he worked. As I savored this lovely memory, my disgust at winter fell away, replaced by a consoling gratitude. I was able to reestablish my enjoyment of winter's wonder, as well as to reenter the goodness of my parents.

That's the power of memory. Not all memories are such pleasant ones, of course. Certain recollections call forth hurtful experiences from the past. My friend's remembrances stirred up anger and resentment about past harmful behavior of a family member. But those memories eventually brought an opportunity to heal her past soreness. Even painful recollections can eventually lead us to be thankful when they engender healing, as Linda Hogan previously indicated.

We do not always have to look backward to find gratitude. We can certainly find it in the present moment by detecting what engages us positively. But much of the time, we need a bit of distance and the ability to recall the past in order to gather our thankfulness. Here is something I wrote some time ago in *The Cup of Our Life*: "Memory can bless us or haunt us, depending on what stirs inside our mind, and how we receive and live with it. Be the gatekeeper of these memories. Catch the ones that draw forth and enhance your core goodness. Savor them. Let these blessed memories fill you with hope."

The poet Emily Dickinson believed, "Such good things can happen to people who learn to remember." With this in mind, here is a suggestion for a November spiritual practice. Pause at the end of each day. Within that quiet space, look for a cherished memory. There is no need to tug at the past. Simply be open and wait to receive what swims to the surface. If a harsh memory happens to come first, acknowledge its presence, and then release it. When a positive memory enters your awareness, welcome it like a golden ❧ nugget. Embrace and savor it. Gather your newly regenerated gratitude and hold it close to your heart.

Forgotten Gifts

In thanksgiving for life, I pledge
to overcome the illusion of entitlement
by reminding myself that everything is gift
and, thus, to live gratefully.

~ Brother David Steindl-Rast

When relatives and friends gather around a table laden with mouth-watering food on Thanksgiving Day, they usually express appreciation for such things as "the food, the cook, good health, freedom, love." I rarely hear thankfulness for other items most of us consider indispensable, such as clean water, garbage collection, electricity, and indoor plumbing. Except for during a natural disaster when we are temporarily deprived of these presumed necessities, it's understandable that by taking these things for granted we would forget they are actually gifts. We assume we have a right to such fundamentals for our living, that they ought to be available for our use at all times. Yet an extensive part of the world's population lives without these essentials and would rejoice to have any one of them. No matter how hard these people work, they are deprived of what is easily accessible to us.

There is another basic gift for which we can neglect to give thanks. If you have the ability to read this, you are one of the fortunate people on our planet. Not because you are reading this particular item, but because of the fact that you can actually read. As of 2020, 115 million youth around the globe were illiterate. Forty-four million adults in the United States were unable to read a simple story to their children. That may be difficult to believe, but these numbers are based on reliable statistics. I discovered this shocking reality when teaching about compassion for marginalized persons. As I prepared my notes, I became acutely conscious of being able to read what was in front of me. Literacy is such a significant part of my life, yet I had ignored this amazing gift by assuming its presence and disregarding what it allowed me to do.

This happens with other benefits, as well. Individual kindness goes unnoticed until a flow of cards and visits arrive during an illness. The support of a community is ignored until a crowd gathers for a special celebration. The same with literacy. One word, one sentence, one page, might not seem like much, but think of the astounding number of words you've read over a lifetime. Imagine just one day when you could not read or write. Consider traveling anywhere without recognizing street signs, not comprehending the information on a bank or medical notice, incapable of perceiving the message received on a mobile phone, unable to read a Bible verse or prayer, inept at trying to help with children's homework, bewildered by the food labels in a supermarket, and powerless to decipher a recipe.

Do you remember who first helped you to read? Can you recall what it felt like to open a book and actually pronounce and understand the words on the page? Perhaps reading did not come readily for you or you had difficulty due to poor eyesight. Or you may be someone who read at an early age and has never stopped relishing the ability to do so. Each of us has our own story of becoming literate. It's a story that has helped shape us into the persons we are today. What would life have been like for us if we had never been able to read? ❍

A tendency exists in our Western society for people who have plenty to think they never have enough. Thanksgiving invites us to look closely at the individual pieces of our lives, to recognize our abundance. Literacy is one of the many things that contributes to this prosperity.

The simplest of things can help me recognize my forgotten gifts like literacy. Several days ago, the office printer died. Of course, it happened on a day when I felt *everything* needed to be printed. I went into a tizzy for a while. Then I remembered there are much bigger issues in life. Having a dead printer soon became less of a nuisance. But what I really learned in the next day or so while I searched for and installed a new machine was my lack of appreciation. Not having the use of the printer made me recognize my daily reliance on it.

A very different situation also led me to think about being grateful for what we have when I attended the funeral of a man who was spouse, father, grandfather, brother, father-in-law, nephew, colleague, and friend. I did not know this man personally, but as I sat among the group gathered to celebrate his life, I wondered if those who loved and respected him had taken his presence for granted. Did they have regrets? Was there more they wished they had been or done for him? Being unmindful of the people we cherish happens without our realizing it, especially in this activity-obsessed society. Only when our dear ones depart from us does the full impact and treasure of their lives become fully apparent. ● Sunset -

Thanks to my printer conking out, I am asking myself some valuable questions. Most of them center around awareness or lack of it. Am I observant of my ability to breathe? Am I cognizant of how great it is to be independent and mobile, to drive a car, to see the landscape? When was the last time I was amazed at being able to hear, to think, to laugh? The questions also pertain to my work— am I valuing my abilities and appreciating the possibilities that work provides? Renewal -

What small things have we overlooked? What individual gifts might we gather as a whole and see with new eyes? What awesome privileges and opportunities do we take for granted? Brother David Steindl-Rast encourages his readers to be thankful for both little and big gifts. He proposes that "gratefulness can be improved by practice."

It's never too late to start.

Spiritual Kinship

I want to go on living after my death.

~ **Anne Frank**

Anne Frank has certainly gone on living long after she died at age fifteen in the Bergen-Belsen concentration camp in 1945. More than thirty million copies of her diary have sold since her death. Not everyone has a published diary like hers to keep their beliefs and values alive in the hearts and minds of those who go on living. But the qualities that inspire and endear others to us hold the potential of remaining influential long after they leave us behind. As I grow older, I feel increasingly in touch with my spiritual ancestors. I believe the appreciation I had for them when they were alive remains firm even though they are no longer physically present.

This type of kinship is not necessarily based on personal ancestry, although it may include people from this lineage. Spiritual kinship consists of characteristics we resonate with that keep us united with the virtues of these ancestors. Kinship of the spirit affirms core beliefs and attitudes. It keeps us attuned to what we consider to be of greatest value and fortifies it. Spiritual kinship motivates us to have similar intrinsic qualities drawn forth from ourselves.

When Sufi writer Kabir Helminski reflects on the "essence of the spiritual process" in *Living Presence,* he names human qualities that reflect the presence of divinity: "Love, generosity, patience, courage, humility, and wisdom." A different listing, by Frank Ostaseski, includes "compassion, strength, peace, clarity, contentment, humility, and equanimity." Of course, the features of kinship cannot be limited to just these few virtues.

195

In *The Five Invitations*, Ostaseksi adds that it can be helpful "to think of these qualities as our inner guidance system, which can lead us to a greater sense of well-being." He believes "we already have everything we need for this journey. It all exists within us. We don't need to be someone special to access our inner qualities and utilize them in the service of greater freedom and transformation." While we do have these characteristics within us, most often they are recognized and empowered with the assistance of others, either directly or indirectly.

Each year the liturgical celebration of All Saints Day in early November leads me to a renewed appreciation for spiritual kinship and how my core goodness has been motivated due to others who entered my life. Ever since my youth, I've felt a connection with certain saints because of their particular virtues. As I've aged, my kindred spirits have expanded to include uncanonized saints—persons I've admired for their selflessness and philosophy of life, people I've known personally and others I've met through literature, history, and various media.

Not long ago, an unexpected conversation at a retreat rekindled the wonder of how spiritual kinship evolves. No one at the breakfast table knew one another. In an attempt to get acquainted with the participants, I casually asked one of them about her profession. This led her to speak of volunteering for three organizations to end the trafficking of children for sex and work. Soon after this, a person from another state revealed that she was a member of a coalition in her city that also aimed to expose and eliminate trafficking. No sooner had she finished when yet another woman from a different area shared how she served as the director of a residence that provided housing for trafficked individuals. At that point, I felt something happening—a unity developing among the three of them that was not there before—sparked by their mutual desire for justice and compassion.

As I left the table that morning, I marveled at how these three women uncovered a commonality in their compassionate service. How astounding that they ended up sitting at the same table. Later, while I walked over to the conference center, memories of similar experiences returned: the two mothers in Illinois who happened to sit next to each other and learned that each of them had a teenage daughter who ran away from home and never returned. It was obvious how these two women immediately drew strength from each other's maternal love and heartache. I've noticed how this unusual situation often happens within groups—people with comparable experiences inadvertently find one another: those who were orphaned when they were quite young, widowed persons, survivors of abuse, recovering addicts, single parents, and so forth. *

How does this happen that people who have known similar situations are drawn toward each other? How is it they discover a supportive kinship through this surprising link? I believe that a knowing presence, a loving Spirit, moves among us, unseen but actively guiding us toward people who can provide support and inspiration for what life requires of us. Much like we are drawn toward a canonized saint we admire, an encounter with these persons comforts, encourages, and motivates us because of their beliefs, values, and experiences. We believe anew that our journey has meaning and worth. And perhaps without being conscious of it at the time, another outgrowth from our soul's central Taproot begins to extend and stretch itself.

This is what has developed for me through the years. I look back and see ever more clearly how certain persons enlivened a dormant goodness in myself. Every year All Saints Day opens the door and invites me to step inside my memory and name those whose admirable qualities have influenced the way I go about my life. • M Theresa

As I have done in the past several years, this November I intend to make a list of the deceased people with whom I've sensed a spiritual kinship. Each day I will write down one of these names and reflect on how I have been affected by this legacy. Then I will hold that name to my heart with renewed appreciation.

I will also ponder questions related to spiritual kinship: How will the way I've chosen to live affect the transformation of those who come after me? Will I have empowered and strengthened these persons to cultivate the best and truest of what is within them? Have I responded to the Holy One in a way that is allowing my life to be a source of spiritual kinship?

Footprints on Our Hearts

Some people come into our lives and leave footprints on our hearts and we are never the same.

~ **Flavia Weedn**

When November arrives, a surge of gratitude comes with it. I relish the thin veil of the Celtic tradition with its assurance that the ancestors approach close by on the eve of October 31. For a short while their spirits greet ours with a mystical presence. The feast of All Saints on the following day also invites us to connect with people of the past who have touched our lives and left lasting marks of goodness.

Whether recognized by the official Church or not, these remarkable "saints" influenced our lives and left their mark on our hearts, much like Flavia Weedn described. As happens now with easy access to the internet, the above, well-known quote of hers has some valuable pieces missing. Here is the more inspiring version: "Some people come into our lives and quickly go. Some people stay for awhile, and move our souls to dance. They awaken us to a new understanding with the passing whisper of their wisdom. Some people make the sky more beautiful to gaze upon. They stay in our lives for awhile, leave footprints on our hearts, and we are never, ever the same."

Since my twenties, I've been aware that who I am and who I am becoming is largely due to people who step onto my path of life long enough to encourage my growth in a particular way. In the past, some have been relatives. Others were strangers. Some visitors have names I no longer remember. And then there are people who come easily to mind. What have they imprinted on my heart? Here are a few of the many gifts that provide purpose and direction for my life: generosity with time and presence, the activation of compassion, trust in my writing ability, access to inner resilience during difficult situations, relishing nature as a place to meet the holy, and choosing to live more contemplatively.

Mark Shields, in his departure as a political analyst on the PBS *Newshour*, was asked about his career as a successful, well-known, and admired figure. He humbly referred to something that his parents taught him, a truth that guided and stayed with him for his entire life, one that influenced his attitude toward his reputation: "Every one of us has been warmed by fires we did not build and every one of us has drunk from wells we did not dig."

Joan Chittister, O.S.B., a central writer on spirituality for many years, reflects the truth of Shield's comment in *The Story of Ruth*, her book about friendship between women: "The fact is that every generation of women forms the next. What one is, the next also will be. What one begins, the other will complete." Chittister adds later in the chapter, "The function of an older generation of women is the empowerment of the next." This statement offers another way of remembering who has left footprints on our hearts—those who have empowered us to be more than we thought we could be.

When we look at what we appreciate most about ourselves and how we've lived, there are usually figures of significance without whose presence we would never have brought forth our individual talents and virtues. Whether young or old, if you allow yourself some quiet time to reflect on who inspired you to grow and share your best, both in the past and on into now, I am confident you will recover memories of persons whose presence assisted your personal transformation, persons whose footprints are as long-lasting as any professional tattoo could be.

- Who has been a positive figure of enrichment and guidance for you?
- Who drew forth from you some of your best qualities that you did not even know were there?
- Who cheered you on when you stepped hesitantly into an unsure future with hope for using your talents?

- Who went on supporting and loving you when you lost your courage?
- Who taught you how to pray and discover a relationship with the divine?
- Who waited with you and encouraged you while you healed?
- Who coaxed you by their compassionate love to see where your falseness hid?
- Who stood by you through the greatest perils and the roughest seas?

We have much for which to be grateful this Thanksgiving. Here is a Thanksgiving Prayer to carry with you as we celebrate each and every person who knowing, or unknowingly, left a significant mark on our lives:

Beloved Presence on the pathway of my life,
thank you for the footprints left on my heart,
the soft and gentle ones that brought comfort,
the deep and lasting ones of enduring friendship,
the lightly passing ones conveying kindness,
the heavy ones leading to necessary change,
and the impressionable footprints swept away
by time or lack of an ability to remember.
Even though lost, forgotten, or not recognized,
these visitors have led me to live more fully
the innate goodness residing within me.
How grateful I am for every footstep of growth
I have taken because others have traveled with me.

November, a Passageway

True surrender, and nothing less, is a certain indication
that one has recognized, finally, one's own vaster and
deeper being, one's own Essential Nature.

~ Kathleen Dowling Singh

As I drove through the Midwest in late summer, the land revealed
a magnificent abundance of fruit, vegetables, and grains. By early
November, these same orchards, gardens, and fields were stripped
of their summer crops. Exposed gardens displayed dried vines and
withered flowers. Orchards gave quick evidence of having been
emptied of their fruitfulness. All that profusion of grain and lush
abundance, gone. What once loudly proclaimed fullness now was
announcing emptiness.

When November arrives, the land enters a transitional phase, a
passageway from a source of plenty to a place of barrenness. The
weary land appears useless and dead, but nutrients in it remain to
be regenerated in the untilled soil. The constant surge of energy
that nature instilled in the land will quietly retain and revitalize
the life-giving elements during slower paced months. The promise of future plenitude hides within what appears to be completely
nonproductive.

We humans also have our seasonal fullness and emptiness. When
our interior summer emerges, life goes extremely well. We feel en-
ergized, industrious, and satisfied. Then as quickly as a machine
robs a golden wheat field of its ripened grain, our contentment can
disappear. What was nurtured and tended gets stripped from us
by something such as a sudden illness, lost spiritual energy, mental
fatigue, a drooping relationship, emotions shoving us out of sync,

devastating societal and world events we feel helpless to change, or any part of life that flattens our spirits or deprives us of satisfaction.

A disconcerting incident can come charging in like a rumbling combine shaving off row after row of treasured grain planted and tended with care. Eckhart Tolle relates a story in *A New Earth* about a schoolteacher with cancer who had months to live. She was coming to peace with her illness and impending death, but one day when Tolle visited, he found her in an agitated state. Her treasure, a diamond ring of her grandmother's, was missing. The schoolteacher felt sure the hired caretaker had stolen it. She seethed with anger and was ready to call the police. Tolle listened to her distress with compassion. Then he asked her to look inside herself and find out how important the ring was at that point in her life. When the distressed woman responded with defensiveness, Tolle looked at her gently and asked, "Do you realize that you will have to let go of the ring, perhaps quite soon? Will you become less when you let go of it?"

After a time of reflection, the distraught woman spoke again. It was obvious she was in touch with her true center when she gave this response: "Suddenly I could feel my I AM-ness. I have never felt that before. If I can feel the I AM so strongly, then who I am hasn't been diminished at all. I can still feel it now, something peaceful but very alive." With this reflection, she was able to let the ring go, and after her death, relatives found the diamond ring in the medicine cabinet.

A distraught experience such as Tolle describes, or any other difficult experience, parallels the harvested land with seemingly little left in it. We may wonder if contentment will ever return. If only we could see this stripping as a time to regenerate the soil of our spirits, to revitalize our trust in a Love that never abandons us, to allow our overactive selves to simply rest for a while in a humbled state of dormancy and be at peace with our I AM-ness. Our seasonal passageway beckons to us: "Come, go slower. Brush the debris from your heart. Empty your mind of its burdens. Look more deeply at your interior life. Discover what wants to be given time to regenerate."

As unappealing as it may seem, this nonproductive and empty stage might actually be an opportunity for gratitude. When we cannot alter the disturbing conditions of what most concerns us, when we feel fully spent and unable to see the light beyond our personal darkness, it is time to step back, to gain some distance from the distress, and give thanks for the invitation to regain perspective. We settle in like the November land and accept what we cannot change. We allow a restorative period to commence for the sources that fed our energy and served to nurture others. We accept the invitation to let go of fretting and accept the posture of relaxing in the abode of quiescence. We trust that a restored vigor will return at a future time yet to be determined.

Harsh and painful situations pose the greatest challenge regarding gratitude. Yet I've known people to locate subtle benefits within hardship and heartache. Just last week I received a note from a friend after her breast cancer surgery: "The inner journey is really what is quite amazing. I have never felt so strongly the power of energy, and prayers and love coming my way, and I pray to stay open and consciously connected to that flow."

After Hurricane Isaac severely flooded areas of Louisiana, the father of a family was interviewed on the evening news. When asked what it was like to no longer have a home, the man turned and motioned toward his wife and children huddled nearby. In a quavering voice he said, "I have what's most important to me." I was deeply touched by that man's response and immediately thought of the scripture verse "Where your treasure is, there your heart will be also" (Mt 6:21).

When catastrophe or major trouble erupts, especially a life-threatening situation such as a close call in a car accident, a near fatal heart attack, or other bodily peril, how quickly life takes on a different hue, whether it happens to us or to someone we count dear. When death brushes by closely, the absolutely necessary items on the calendar become much less important. For a while the nit-picky irritations, the grumbles and gripes, are also set aside. We have each other. We have life. We can go on. How fortunate we are. We realize anew where our treasure is.

We continually relearn to appreciate what we value, to trust that the emptying time will be followed with the arrival of some fresh life currently hiding itself. Our I AM-ness will live on. In each of us there resides a gift for our growth through every passageway that arrives.

Gratitude for Hidden Ones

Inner Vision of Souls,
release the cataracts on my heart
to reveal the people I fail to see
and those I automatically ignore
even when they are in plain sight—
the hidden ones who make my life
livable, comfortable, doable.

This morning I look across the wide expanse
of the parking lot to the sidewalk beyond;
a lone, heavy-coated figure at 6:00 a.m.
strews deicer on the path to the office building,
an unnoticed but significant gesture
that can protect a limb from quickly breaking.

These hidden ones collect garbage in pre-dawn,
clean messy hotel rooms and deliver our food.
They watch the skies for incoming planes
and guard the safety of our cities and homes.
They take temperatures, adjust ventilators,
and transport strangers here and there.

Do I ever pause to offer thanks for them?
Do I even consider their existence?
How changed my life would be
were they to end the service they provide.

Morning arrives. The hidden ones go home
or maybe they just begin to start their day.
As they do so, Safe Harbor of Hidden Ones,
hold them close to your compassionate love.

~ Joyce Rupp

December

The four weeks of Advent lead us inward to our sacred Taproot. We imbibe of the nourishment that comes from stillness and an awareness of the human sanctuaries in which Love dwells. We celebrate this incarnated Love in the form of Jesus as the most precious gift beneath the tree of life. Once again Emmanuel fills our hearts with welcome gladness.

Receiving from the Taproot

Five disciplined days of retreat,
sitting in soundless contemplation,
rising in the sunless dawn, content
with December's inaudible voice.
Slowly absorbing a gauzy presence,
a womb-like embrace of the sacred
where I can simply be with this love,
without interruptive word or thought.

Nothing more, nothing less than that.

I do not need to produce a thing.
I do not long to have a great insight.
I do not have to have good feelings.
Just sit in the Advent waiting room,
joining an eternal hush in the silent soil
of winter's dormant heart.

I rest. Reenergize. Quietly rejoicing
in the hollow of this muted prayer,
a loving space that cradles my spirit,
easing tired fibers and gladly receiving
nourishment from the beloved Taproot.

What more could I want?

~ **Joyce Rupp**

208

A Living Sanctuary

There is a special shelter around every person. That shelter is the shelter of your soul, it is the shelter of your God, and it is the shelter of your angel.

~ John O'Donohue

When I stay overnight at my community's motherhouse in Omaha, Nebraska, some evenings I slip into the chapel after most everyone has retired. As soon as I walk into the darkened space I feel a welcoming presence meeting my spirit, a comforting balm. With only the flickering sanctuary lamp to keep me company, I am wrapped in a sheltering peace. This chapel and other spaces that are quietly prayed in carry an aura of secure serenity. Little spaces in homes set aside for reflection, counseling offices that provide a safe space to heal, bedsides of the dying where hushed reverence prevails, certain peace-laden areas in nature—these and similar places offer a refuge for us when we desire to be welcomed without expectation of being anything other than who we are.

Our inner self can also be a sanctuary. Catherine T. Nerney relates an incident regarding this kind of shelter. In *The Compassion Connection*, she tells how a "wise and loving father" sat down with each of his almost-teenage sons and used the word "sanctuary" to assure them that they would always be welcomed by him, no matter what they had done. He spoke of future mistakes and actions his sons might regret and their fear of the consequences. He went on to assure them, "When that happens, please. . . . Come to me and say only *sanctuary* and I will know. You can sit there in the silence, and I will keep you sheltered by a love that will never let you go, no matter what you did. We will get through it together. I want you to know this now and to count on it when you feel despondent, like a failure and want to run away. I will be your sanctuary—till you can carry on."

Wow, I thought, *have I ever been that fully accepting of another person, or even of myself? Can I embrace this father's kind of welcome?* It may be that offering sanctuary to ourselves is the most difficult welcome of all, the kind found in Parker Palmer's *On the Brink of Everything*: "Sanctuary is wherever I find a safe space to regain my bearings, reclaim my soul, heal my wounds, and return to the world as a wounded healer. It's not merely about finding shelter from the storm—it's about spiritual survival and the capacity to carry on."

Interior sanctuary implies having what is essential to continue life's journey, even when feeling lost, uncertain, insecure, or depleted of hope. The notion of sanctuary abounds in the Advent season. Zechariah and Elizabeth received Mary into their home for almost three months. While there and when she was back home in Nazareth, Mary provided a safe sanctuary for Jesus in her womb. When Joseph and Mary traveled from their home they found refuge in the place where Jesus was born. Later, when this family fled as refugees from violence, they sought a sanctuary of protection in the foreign land of Egypt.

I didn't have sanctuary on my mind when I took part in an Advent retreat, but that topic leapt out at me soon after the facilitator invited us to choose one of the art pieces strewn across the large table to use for our meditation. I selected a painting directly in front of me by D. A. Siqueiros titled *Peasant Mother*. I spent the next hour or so reflecting on it. The peasant mother stands solid as granite, her feet planted firmly between two tall saguaro cacti, their thick arms stretching upward amid a bleak surrounding. The broad-shouldered woman bends her right leg, the left one slightly forward, as if to balance the weight of the child held closely within her embracing cloak.

The peasant mother completely enfolds the slumbering child within her two strong, round arms, the fingers of her hands intertwined as if locked together for support and protection. Clearly this scene depicts a devoted haven of safety. A mother cradles her child in the wilderness, a maternal sanctuary for this innocent one who knows not the smell of danger or the fierceness of hatred; instead, this little one gently rests in the mother's protective mantle.

I especially observed the mother's wide face, a replica of expansive love turned toward her child, so close that her nose and lips touch his cheek. Her obvious intent of providing a loving sanctuary nurtured a desire in me to be there for people who have lost a sense of belonging, for those whose strenuous journey has drained hope and passion for the future, leaving the residue of a weakened determination to survive.

After I closed my meditation, I longed to be like the mother, embracing those seeking shelter, touching the flesh of my prayer to the cheeks of destitution and despair. The words of social activist Dorothy Day added to that desire: "All Christians are called to be hospitable, but it is more than serving a meal or filling a bed, opening our door—it is to open ourselves, our hearts, to the needs of others." I wanted to be a voice for the voiceless in the wilderness of migration, for refugees longing to know the security of a home, to offer lonely persons the embrace of warm, round arms of acceptance and the cloak of unconditional love. I felt called to be a living sanctuary in any way that I could.

As I left the retreat that day, I knew I could not travel to where immigrants waited at the borders to be allowed in. I could not go to refugee camps far away. But I was sure that I would have countless opportunities to kindle the coals of generous compassion and kindness into blazing gifts of welcome, to carry this unreserved hospitality outward to others by having a welcoming heart for whomever I met. And I could speak up for those needing refuge along with seeking legislation for those requiring sanctuary and a legal welcome. How much I could offer would depend on how generous I decided to be with my time and care and on how much compassion I would allow to come forth from myself.

As the season of Advent opens, I invite each of you to join me in being a *living sanctuary*, to be more than just a momentary kindness given to another. We can become a consistent, welcoming presence assuring others that they are safe from impatience, nonacceptance, self-centeredness, and intolerance when they pass through the borders of our hearts.

A Deeper Seeing

And now here is my secret, a very simple secret: It is only with the heart that one can see rightly; what is essential is invisible to the eye.

~ Antoine de Saint-Exupéry

The familiar quote above from *The Little Prince* encompasses a wealth of counsel. It encourages us to live at a deeper level instead of skimming the surface in our too-hurried patterns of living, especially in the eventful weeks preceding Christmas. Experiencing life below the radar, in the realm of the heart, means not only decreasing our speed but also being attentive to what rests within the veiled layers of those we love.

Jungian therapist Helen Luke refers to this way of seeing when she reflects on Laurens van der Post's writings about the San Bushmen in the Kalahari desert of Botswana: "I remember the ancient greeting of the Bushman . . . which is always 'I see you.' How beautiful and profound that is! Not a question—'How do you do?'—or a conventional wish—'Good morning'—but simply a statement that the individual is *seeing* another unique person, seeing his essence, not his qualities good or bad. . . . The greeting 'I see you'—if one could use it not only to every person but to every *thing* one meets."

"I see you" came home to me in a poignant and evocative way when I made a trip to Kansas to visit a friend who had lung cancer. We had sparse contact with each other for a number of years, and I sensed our visit would be a special one. Little did I know how special. When I arrived in Topeka, I learned that Ken's wife, Bibi, had taken him to the emergency room that morning because of severe chest pains. I hurriedly drove to the hospital hoping we could have some quality time together. I found Ken to be as I remembered: gentle, optimistic, gregarious, loving, and faith-filled. Fortunately, he had not lost his sly sense of humor either.

When I was readying to say goodbye, Ken asked if he could take a picture of me and if I would stand at the foot of his bed while he did so. Being a bit puzzled because he was not holding a camera, I hesitantly proceeded to do as he requested. "There," he chuckled, "just perfect." Then he asked me if I would stand there quietly. As I did so, Ken gazed at my face with a soft smile. In turn, I gazed back at him. That's how we "took photos" of one another.

As I looked in silence at Ken's face, my gaze moved to focus on his eyes. It was as if I could enter the light there and see far beyond his physical being, to a sphere of pure love, to his essence. The concept of "I see you" became real in that moment. When the brief "photo taking" was over, Ken thanked me. I responded, "I'm awed. I think there was a moment when I glimpsed your soul." I know he understood.

I did not find it comfortable at first, just standing there, being seen. This seems sort of ridiculous, but I admit to feeling a slight embarrassment and a disquieting vulnerability. Having my "photo taken" in that manner required more than my physical self be revealed. Perhaps that is why I, and many others, hurry through our days instead of standing still long enough to "see what is invisible to the eye," to discover and treasure what is essential and lasting within the essence of ourselves and others.

After I returned home, I sent Ken a note affirming his beautiful, loving approach to remembering a friend. Here is the email I received in return: "I got out of the hospital on Saturday, and every now and then I take your picture out and look at it. I did not wear it out though, and I cannot lose it. I can look at it anytime, even in the dentist's chair. He never says a word. He just keeps drilling."

Later that week Ken sent me another note when I asked him if I could share his "taking a picture" with my readers. "Sure, Joyce, you can use that simple little picture thing. It's easy. Flowers are great subjects. Just take a time exposure in your mind. Close your eyes. Review your picture with the real subject and it is secured. Once in a while you can take out your album for review. And at night you can get lots of memories, laughs, and good times. Human subjects are best. It has to be a time exposure though or it doesn't work. No copyright rules apply. Oh, I forgot. Beginners should avoid time exposures of wild beasts and advancing tornadoes."

It's been five years since Ken's death. Because of that precious experience we had when we took photos of each other with our eyes, I can still see him in my mind's eye. Ken is as clear as can be, lying there in his hospital bed, the look of love shining from his face. That is the beauty of the photos we take with the cameras of our ✷ hearts.

People's physical appearance, especially their eyes, allows us to be in touch with them when we behold them with reverence. I have sometimes heard the comment in the years after a person's death, "I've forgotten what he (or she) looked like." Material photos serve as a reminder, but that is not enough. We need the light in our loved one's eyes. We need that deeper seeing which death steals from us—unless we have taken "time exposures in our mind."

When we gather with our dear ones this Christmas and it's time for photo-taking, let it be a reminder to also take a long, loving look with the eyes of our heart.

What Are You Asking for This Christmas?

Instead of focusing on material presents, why not ask from the Heart of the Holy what most rejuvenates our spirits and enriches our truest selves? Here are the gifts I am requesting:

Love
to be the north star in my soul,
leading me always in the direction of divine Light.

Stillness
to sweep through my restless mind,
instilling calmness and a serenity that dispels apprehension.

Nonviolence
to enter every thought, word, deed, and desire,
flowing gently from me like a brook caressing inflexible stones.

Savoring
to remember with thankfulness
lovely moments of beauty and the joy of people's goodwill.

Other-Centeredness
to dissolve the closely held part of myself
that prefers to ignore or refuse to respond to the plight of others.

Laughter
to retain the sprightly dance of joy
amid endless duties, preparations, chores, and responsibilities.

Perspective
to expand an inner vision that sees
each difficult person or situation through the wide lens of kindness.

Solace
to recognize, welcome, and embrace
whoever or whatever seeks shelter in the sanctuary of self.

Hope
to rekindle my affection and gratitude
for the Source of Love who intermingles with each part of my life.

~ Joyce Rupp

An Expanded Heart

In the seasons of our Advent—waking, working, eating, sleeping, being—each breath is a breathing of Christ into the world.

~ **Caryll Houselander**

Carmen Lampe Zeitler relates a beautiful story in a Children and Family Urban Ministries newsletter. She tells of a five-year-old boy named Emilio drawing a stick-figure of a tall black man and a small brown boy. When asked about it, he explained, "I wish that I could meet Martin Luther King Jr." Last year Emilio was in sixth grade and traveled with other children to Simpson College to take part in a march to end "-isms," such as racism, sexism, and classism. To Emilio's surprise, the story picture he drew when he was five was shown to the gathered crowd. Later, Emilio held the picture close to his chest and exclaimed, "I can't believe I did this. I must have had an expanded heart!"

An expanded heart—I resonate with that phrase and what it implies: a sense of something much bigger than ourselves, a wide embrace of another, room enough within one's self to extend a welcome without regard for color, class, or creed. *An expanded heart* is going to be my motivation during this Advent season as I renew my desire to welcome Christ in every person. I hope my heart can grow wide enough to be hospitable, open enough to accept those different from me, generous enough to do what it takes to be kind, and large enough to spontaneously extend compassion.

This won't be easy. In her Advent book *Night Visions*, Jan Richardson refers to a story Kathleen Norris conveyed about an old monk trained to welcome every guest as another Christ. He told a younger

218

monk, "I have finally learned to accept people as they are. Whatever they are in the world, a prostitute, a prime minister, it is all the same to me. But sometimes I see a stranger coming up the road and I say, 'Oh, Jesus Christ, is it you again?'"

Richardson continues, "Those who welcomed Jesus—the angels, the shepherds, the Magi—readily recognized him and knew the import of his arrival. They greeted him joyfully with their songs, their presence, their gifts. The rest of us sometimes have a more difficult time welcoming Christ into our midst, particularly when he arrives in the guise of one who seems radically different from us or who gets under our skin or who angers us or who confronts us with parts of ourselves we don't want to see."

Genuine hospitality implies being considerate and choosing to be nonjudgmental—which requires allowing another to enter the room of our hearts without a lot of preconditions. I think of the welcome of Mary's womb where she nourished Love into human form. Advent today is not about preparing for the coming of the physical Jesus. Mary's yes provided that welcome for us. However, the Spirit of Love in this human child who arrived long ago remains fully alive. Advent invites us to reawaken our awareness of this mystical presence, to welcome Christ in those who show up wherever we are.

What this means for me is a daily renewal and intention to be truly open. This resolve challenges my judgments, loosens my grip on my grudges, and requires me to reorient my heart toward certain individuals and groups. Because of this intention, I have placed one word on my prayer altar this Advent: *accept*. It's a small word with a big potential. If I really live this word formed of six simple letters, it could change significantly how I experience both Advent and Christmas.

It is one thing to accept strangers. It is quite another to be willing to invite them into our lives. That truly takes an expanded heart. Decades ago when my religious community welcomed a Vietnamese woman named Thuy and her three small children, it was easy for us to greet them every day. But it was Sister Joy who took on the daily tasks of getting them settled in the small house on our property, making sure they had food that agreed with their Asian diet, helping them learn English, and teaching them how to use a washing machine and other modern appliances. Morning, noon, and night Sister Joy's expanded heart was there for them. She spent every bit of her time in resettling the refugees.

Marilyn Lacey also knew what it was like to do this when she engaged in her demanding work with refugee camps in Asia and Africa. In *This Flowing Toward Me*, Lacey looks back on those years and tells of coming across a Rumi poem titled "The Music." In the poem, Rumi describes himself as God's guest and how this divine love has continually flowed into his life even though he has failed to remember it. After reading this poem, Marilyn Lacey understood that during those years she welcomed refugees, God was there welcoming her. She was both the host and the guest.

Rumi's description of what it is like to be the guest certainly speaks to my life. For more than thirty years I've experienced the hospitality of strangers as I traveled continually to lead retreats and speak at conferences. My hosts' thoughtful efforts to provide for my needs and make sure that I felt at ease where I stayed filled me with humble gratitude. I knew there was no way I could adequately return their magnanimous kindness. It was a matter of recognizing and receiving what they offered, and going forth to try to pay it forward.

This kind of hospitality of heart resides at the center of the meeting of Jacob and his brother Esau after Jacob stole the family inheritance from his brother. After many years of this betrayal, Jacob longed to receive his brother's forgiveness. He traveled with trepidation to ask this of Esau. Unbeknownst to Jacob, his brother's heart had also expanded. When Jacob approached to beg forgiveness, Esau "ran to meet him, and embraced him, and fell on his neck and kissed him, and they wept." Then Jacob spoke these beautiful words to his brother: "To see your face is like seeing the face of God—since you have received me with such favor" (see Gn 33:1–11).

If we could carry in our hearts the words Jacob spoke to his brother, our Advent would grow in depth and quality. We each have an ability within ourselves to expand our welcome of others, to see "the face of God" abiding there.

Stillness

Can't you see me standing before you
cloaked in stillness?

~ Rainer Maria Rilke

The weeks before Christmas are usually overloaded with all sorts of activity that keeps our bodies and spirits buzzing. No wonder there's an attraction to Christmas songs referring to a hush and a stillness. As far back as the nineteenth century, the Austrian Christmas carol "Silent Night" and the lullaby, "Still, Still, Still," enthralled the hearts of Christians. These songs connecting stillness with Christmas continue to appeal to many today.

And yet, if we were there at the time of Jesus' birth in the environment of a stable as Luke's gospel describes, it could hardly have been a hushed, silent night. The air would have filled with the gasps and moans of Mary giving birth to her son. Joseph most surely would have been heard comforting and encouraging his wife. If animals were nearby, their bleating, chewing, and mooing contributed to the sound, along with the rustling of their bodies. From outside, the conversation and movement of villagers would have drifted into the birthing place.

To attempt to convince people to slow down, to enter into silence and turn off the noise during Advent might be a lost cause. External silence isn't always possible due to constant activity. Office parties and get-togethers with family and friends, shopping, decorating, and other Christmas preparations cause external stillness to be somewhat elusive, but inner stillness is always available if we are intentional about claiming it.

After I read *Stillness Is the Key* by Ryan Holiday, I had a different take on how to move through Advent when it comes to being spiritually reflective and receptive. I realized that there is a difference between *silence* and *stillness*. Silence relates to the *external* environment—an absence of sound or a lessening of it—while stillness has to do with our *internal* environment. Ryan writes about stillness as the inner space in which we are in harmony with "the mind, the heart, and the body." He insists that stillness must be found and maintained in order to live peacefully.

Stillness is essential to embrace the true spirit of Advent and Christmas. One of the best expressions of stillness comes from Catherine Ingram, who writes in *Passionate Presence*: "In the deepest recesses of ourselves there is a most familiar quietude. It has been there through all our seeking and craving, as well as all the other events of our lives. It is a point of peace, a silent witnessing that is fundamentally unperturbed no matter what happens. Steeping in this awareness, one is at ease in the present, fully welcoming what comes and fully releasing what goes—feeling alive throughout. This awareness is not something far away and in another time. It is already occurring right there and right now."

We might not be able to shut out the sounds coming from our outer lives but we can welcome the quiet of our inner ones. Every morning when I enter my formal time of prayer and meditation I learn the difference between silence and stillness. I almost always have silence—a lack of noise in my room. More rarely do I experience stillness—the ease within the mind and heart where peace floats comfortably. When I meditate in silence, there's often an insistent clatter and chatter filling my brain. But then, there are those precious, unplanned, uncontrolled moments in silence when stillness enters my deeper self—an embrace of Holy Presence that settles and hushes what usually blabbers away in me.

I first recognized the difference between silence and stillness when a middle-aged widow stood before me at a retreat and, in angry voice, questioned why I had invited the group into a period of silence. "I have more than enough of that at home," she informed me. "What I need are people to talk to." I heard the loneliness that was beneath her comment. She was raging against external silence and unable to locate the internal quiet that could ease her hurt, pain, and grief. She had not yet accepted the space of outer silence as a way to gift herself with inner stillness. Her grief was too strong for that.

Silence can evoke loneliness, but it also provides the environment for a stillness to develop in us, one that leads to a peaceful communion. Some folks can rush around during the weeks prior to Christmas and consciously maintain a steadfast peacefulness. Others hurry and scurry with their tasks and find themselves frustrated, irritated, and at odds with themselves and others. What creates the difference?

Rachelle Linner offers an answer: "Advent allows us the holy leisure to immerse ourselves in Scripture, to allow our roots to settle deep into the rich loam that lets us discern the good that God wills for us. It doesn't require feats of memorization, only a heart longing for God, a heart that responds to God's longing for us. We need to do so little. We receive so much."

The "little" we need to do in order to sustain stillness in ourselves, when there is not much external silence, has to do with our willingness to select some "holy leisure." We pause and rest with the Holy One before leaping into the day. We allow ourselves some reflection—maybe a prayer for intentionally walking with the Beloved Companion, a short meditation, or some inspiring reading. The noise within us lessens and the quiet within us then expands.

I've been an admirer of blue herons for a long time. I've learned a lot about stillness by observing them. Herons can be standing by the edge of a river with loud motorboats, flocks of cawing crows, and music blaring from picnickers' loud speakers close by, and the heron is not fazed by it. Amid this external noise, the heron remains completely attentive and focused. Inner stillness reigns with the heron, who chooses to focus on the task at hand. So, too, with us. Our true preparation for Christmas is the task of stilling our minds and hearts to welcome the harmonious love available to us through the presence of the Prince of Peace.

Three Prayers to Carry You through Advent

How often do we fail to see what's right in front of us simply because we're not looking for it?

~ Alice Camille

Holy One, Essence of Kindness, awaken my inner eye to notice how you reveal yourself through thoughtful deeds, to be alert to where and how your kindness is expressed in myself and others. Let me not miss these simple and quickly-shelved manifestations. Each day of this Advent season guide me to your loving affirmation through messages of hope, easy smiles, opened doors, unexpected generosity, words of understanding, forgiving hearts, and other sources of human kindness. Lead me to recognize each gesture as a confirmation of how you dwell among us.

O Come, O Come Emmanuel,
and ransom captive Israel.

~ Seventeenth-century Christian hymn

Emmanuel, God-with-us, you have already come as divinity in human disguise. It is we who are to "come," to draw near to you. It is we who are to be ransomed, to move toward freedom from the armored biases that form around our overly-protected hearts. Move us away from a tendency to join the destructive negativity that infiltrates our troubled society and personal relationships. Help us to out-distance the layers of adverse judgment that prevent us from welcoming those whom we determine as "the other." Come, yes, come Emmanuel, and ransom us. Free us from whatever imprisons our love and prevents us from being a welcoming presence.

> Inside everyone
> is a great shout of joy
> waiting to be born.

> **~ David Whyte**

Awakener of Gladness, a song of jubilant tidings like that of the Bethlehem angels awaits a birth within the marrow of my soul. Sadly, this joy often lies hidden because I am too absorbed in over-ly-scheduled days. This Advent I will allow your transparent joy to fill my heart, to let it course through the hurry and scurry of my activities and slow me down so that I enjoy the gift of being alive. I will remember the happiness associated with your birth and the enduring teachings you gave to our world. I pray with confidence for your joy to continue to be birthed within me and to be shared with those who gather this Christmas.

Acknowledgments

Every publication of mine eventually comes together because it has been touched in some way by the assistance of other people. *Return to the Root* is no exception. While it is impossible to name everyone, I call to mind the following with immense gratitude.

When I've longed for a place of beauty and solitude in which to write, these gracious benefactors have provided one for me: Lynn Barnett; Tim and Trudy Barry; Benedictine Sisters of the House of Bread Monastery at Nanaimo, British Columbia; Bobbi Bussan, O.S.B., and Benet House in Rock Island, Illinois; Trish Herbert; Cedars of Peace in Nerinx, Kentucky; Rivendell on Bowen Island, British Columbia; Spirit in the Desert in Carefree, Arizona; and Villa Maria del Mar in Santa Cruz, California.

As I edited the newsletters, I became aware of how the following were catalysts for my writing through their ideas, resources, stories, and prayer: Janet Barnes, Kathi Bentall, Sr. Mary Anna Callewaert, Cindy Chicoine, Joan Doherty, Mary and Chuck Kunkel, Marks McAvity, Judy Porter, Kathy Quinn, Sr. Ginny Silvestri, Sr. Brenda Rose Szegedy, Brynn White, and Carmen Lampe Zeitler.

Jackie Ryan, prioress of my religious community—the Servants of Mary—has cheered me on by her constant interest and encouragement.

Always I am indebted to the staff at Sorin Books/Ave Maria Press for their expert care in guiding my book into publication. I'm especially indebted to Amber Elder whose keen eyes and wisdom have edited the manuscript, Heather Glenn for her skilled marketing, Karey Circosta, Stephanie Sibal, Kristen Hornyak Bonelli, and Brian C. Conley for their support and work on behalf of *Return to the Root*.

Thanks to Michael Leach, an original version of the essay "Gaze and Be Amazed" was first published in his column "Soul Seeing" in *The National Catholic Reporter*, October, 2011.

Bibliography

Introduction

Helminski, Kabir. *Living Presence: A Sufi Way to Mindfulness & the Essential Self.* New York: TarcherPerigee, 1992.

Main, John. *The Way of Unknowing: Expanding Spiritual Horizons Through Meditation.* Norwich, UK: Canterbury Press, 2012.

Underhill, Evelyn. *Essential Writings.* New York: Orbis Books, 2003.

January

Alam Fakrul, and Radha Chakravarty, eds. *The Essential Tagore.* Boston: Belknap Press, 2014.

Moore, Kathleen Dean. *Holdfast: At Home in the Natural World.* Guilford, CA: Lyons Press, 1999.

Taylor, Jill Bolte. *My Stroke of Insight: A Brain Scientist's Personal Journey.* New York: Penguin, 2009.

Wiederkehr, Macrina. *Seven Sacred Pauses: Living Mindfully Through the Hours of the Day.* Notre Dame, IN: Sorin Books, 2010.

February

Coelho, Paulo. *The Spy: A Novel of Mata Hari.* New York: Vintage Books, 2017.

Francl-Donnay, Michelle. "Fashioned to be Generous." *Give Us This Day* (November 26, 2020): 270.

Hays, Edward. *A Book of Wonders: Daily Reflections for Awakened Living.* Notre Dame, IN: Ave Maria Press, 2009.

Kornfield, Jack. *A Path With Heart: A Guide Through the Perils and Promises of Spiritual Life.* New York: Bantam Books, 1993.

Lamott, Anne. *Almost Everything: Notes on Hope.* New York: Riverhead Books, 2018.

Lewis, C. S. *The Four Loves.* New York: HarperOne, 2017.

Rutter, E. Jane. *Give Us This Day* (June 17, 2020): 188–89.

Shapiro, Rami. *The Sacred Art of LovingKindness: Preparing to Practice.* Nashville: SkyLight Paths Publishing, 2006.

Whyte, David. *Consolations: The Solace, Nourishment and Underlying Meaning of Everyday Words.* Langley, WA: Many Rivers Press, 2015.

March

Bangley, Bernard, ed. *The Cloud of Unknowing.* Orleans, MA: Paraclete Press, 2006.

Boorstein, Sylvia. "About Practice, Clear Seeing, and Keeping the Faith," in *The Fabric of the Future: Women Visionaries of Today Illuminate the Path to Tomorrow.* Edited by M.J. Ryan. Newburyport, MA: Conari Press, 2000.

Dass, Ram. *Polishing the Mirror: How to Live from Your Spiritual Heart.* Louisville, CO: Sounds True, 2014.

Francis. "Welcome the Light of God." *Give Us This Day* (November 1, 2020): 24.

Julian of Norwich. *Enfolded in Love.* London: Darton, Longman & Todd, 2004.

Melville, Marilyn. *Longing, Belonging.*

Merton, Thomas. *New Seeds of Contemplation.* New York: New Directions, 2007.

Pope, Victoria. "Waiting for Gdansk." *National Geographic* (September 2020): 136.

Smith, Cyprian. *The Way of Paradox: Spiritual Life as Taught by Meister Eckhart.* London: Darton, Longman & Todd, 2004.

Smith, Emile Teresa. "The Stubborn Witness of a Revolutionary Poet," *Sojourners* (March 2020): 23–27.

Wicks, Robert. *Night Call: Embracing Compassion and Hope in a Troubled World.* Oxford, UK: Oxford University Press, 2017.

April

Dalai Lama, Desmond Tutu, and Douglas Adams. *The Book of Joy.* New York: Avery, 2016.

Feldman, Christina. *Boundless Heart: The Buddha's Path of Kindness, Compassion, Joy, and Equanimity.* Berkeley: Shambhala, 2017.

Goldberg, Natalie. "Waking Up to Happiness." *Shambhala Sun* (July 2012).

Liebenson, Narayan Helen. *The Magnanimous Heart: Compassion and Love, Loss and Grief, Joy and Liberation.* Boston: Wisdom Publications, 2019.

Oliver, Mary. "Don't Hesitate," in *Swan: Poems and Prose Poems.* Boston: Beacon Press, 2012.

———. "Mindful," in *Why I Wake Early: New Poems.* Boston: Beacon Press, 2005.

Rupp, Joyce. *The Cup of Our Life: A Guide to Spiritual Growth.* Notre Dame, IN: Ave Maria Press, 2012.

———. *Fresh Bread: And Other Gifts of Spiritual Nourishment.* Notre Dame, IN: Ave Maria Press, 2006.

Sexton, Anne. "Welcome Morning," *The Complete Poems: Anne Sexton.* Boston, MA: Mariner Books, 1999.

Tolle, Eckhart. *The Power of Now: A Guide to Spiritual Enlightenment.* Novato, CA: New World Library, 2004.

May

Adyashanti, *Falling into Grace: Insights on the End of Suffering.* Louisville, CO: Sounds True, 2013.

Brach, Tara. *Radical Compassion: Learning to Love Yourself and Your World with the Practice of RAIN.* New York: Penguin, 2020.

Chittister, Joan. *In Search of Belief.* Liguori, MO: Liguori, 2006.

Chödrön, Pema. *Comfortable with Uncertainty: 108 Teachings on Cultivating Fearlessness and Compassion.* Berkeley: Shambhala, 2018.

———. *When Things Fall Apart: Heart Advice for Difficult Times.* Berkeley: Shambhala, 2016.

DeMello, Anthony. *The Song of the Bird.* New York: Image Books, 1984.

Doyle, Brian. *A Book of Uncommon Prayer:100 Celebrations of the Miracle & Muddle of the Ordinary.* Notre Dame, IN: Ave Maria Press, 2014.

Ford-Grabowsky, Mary. *Stations of the Light: Renewing the Ancient Christian Practice of the Via Lucis as a Spiritual Tool for Today.* New York: Image Books, 2005.

Guinup, Erin. "Everyone Has a Song—Welcoming Refugees Through Music." www.youtube.com/watch?v=8m50VAD_Jp8.

Merrill, Nan C. *Psalms for Praying: An Invitation to Wholeness.* New York: Continuum, 2006.

Moore, Kathleen Dean. *Holdfast: At Home in the Natural World.* Corvallis, OR: Oregon State University Press, 2013.

O'Donohue, John. *Walking in Wonder: Eternal Wisdom for a Modern World.* New York: Convergent Books, 2018.

Smith, Cyprian. *The Way of Paradox: Spiritual Life as Taught by Meister Eckhart.* London: Darton, Longman & Todd, 2004.

Stendl-Rast, David. "Spirituality as Common Sense," https://gratefulness.org/resource/dsr-common-sense.

June

"The Feather: A Symbol of High Honor." https://blog.nativehope.org/the-feather-symbol-of-high-honor.

Gold, Taro. *Living Wabi-Sabi: The True Beauty of Your Life.* Kansas City: Andrews McMeel, 2007.

"How Do Babies Breathe in the Womb?" *Healthline.* www.healthline.com/health/pregnancy/how-babies-breathe-in-the-womb#fetal-breathing-practice.

Kotler, Arnold, ed. *The Thich Nhat Hanh Collection.* New York: One Spirit Press, 2004.

Nepo, Mark. *More Together Than Alone: Discovering the Power and Spirit of Community in Our Lives and in the World.* New York: Atria Books, 2019.

Norris, Gunilla. *Simple Ways: Towards the Sacred.* New York: BlueBridge, 2011.

O'Donohue, John. *Anam Cara: A Book of Celtic Wisdom.* New York: Harper Perennial, 1998.

Rupp, Joyce. *Dear Heart Come Home: The Path of Midlife Spirituality.* New York: Crossroad, 1996.

Sardello, Robert. *Silence: The Mystery of Wholeness.* Berkeley: North Atlantic Books, 2008.

July

"Alan Alda Is Obsessed With the Power of Science." *AARP* newsletter (June/July 2020), 79.

Blackie, Sharon. *The Enchanted Life: Unlocking the Magic of the Everyday.* Toronto: Ambrosia, 2018.

Deignan, Kathleen, ed. *A Book of Hours: Thomas Merton.* Notre Dame, IN: Sorin Books, 2007.

Kelley, Thomas. *A Testament of Devotion.* New York: HarperOne, 1996.

Lesser, Elizabeth. *Marrow: Love, Loss, and What Matters Most.* New York: Harper Wave, 2017.

Martin, James. *My Life With the Saints.* Chicago: Loyola Press, 2006.

Norris, Gunilla. *Simple Ways: Towards the Sacred.* New York: BlueBridge, 2011.

van der Post, Laurens. *The Heart of the Hunter: Customs and Myths of the African Bushman.* San Diego: Harcourt Brace Jovanovich, 1980.

August

Bourgeault, Cynthia. *The Wisdom Way of Knowing: Reclaiming an Ancient Tradition to Awaken the Heart.* San Francisco: Jossey-Bass, 2003.

Fronsdale, Gil. "Upekkha." https://www.insightmeditationcenter.org.

Haughton, Rosemary Luling. "New Heaven and New Earth." *Give Us This Day* (November 27, 2020), 279.

Julian of Norwich. *Revelations of Divine Love.* New York: Dover Publications, 2006.

Lubich, Chiara. "From God's Viewpoint." *Give Us This Day* (September 11, 2020), 117.

Mueller, Wayne. *How Then Shall We Live? Four Simple Questions That Reveal the Beauty and Meaning of Our Lives.* New York: Bantam, 1997.

Nepo, Mark. *Seven Thousand Ways to Listen: Staying Close to What Is Sacred.* New York: Atria Books, 2013.

Salzberg, Sharon. "Calm in the Midst of Chaos." *Lions Roar* (November 2020), 48

Silf, Margaret. *Close to the Heart: A Guide to Personal Prayer.* Chicago: Loyola Press, 2003.

Whitman, Walt. "Song of the Open Road." https://www.poetryfoundation.org/poems/48859/song-of-the-open-road.

September

Boyle, Gregory. *Barking to the Choir: The Power of Radical Kinship.* New York: Simon & Schuster, 2018.

Camille, Alice. *Give Us This Day* (September 2020).

Halifax, Joan. *Standing at the Edge: Finding Freedom Where Fear and Courage Meet.* New York: Flatiron Books, 2019.

Houselander, Caryll. *The Reed of God.* Notre Dame, IN: Christian Classics, 2006.

Lachman, Barbara, ed. *The Journal of Hildegard of Bingen.* New York: Harmony, 1993.

Nepo, Mark. *Seven Thousand Ways to Listen: Staying Close to What Is Sacred.* New York: Atria Books, 2013.

Power, Marjorie. "The Accolade." In *Oncoming Halos.* American Fork, UT: Kelsay Books, 2018.

Pradervand, Pierre. *The Gentle Art of Blessing: Simple Practice That Will Transform You and Your World.* New York: Atria Books, 2009.

Teresa. *Come Be My Light: The Private Writings of the Saint of Calcutta.* Edited by Brian Kolodiejchuk. New York: Image, 2009.

Underhill, Evelyn. "The House of the Soul." In *Essential Writings: Evelyn Underhill.* New York: Orbis Books, 2003.

October

Arrien, Angeles. *The Four-Fold Way: Walking the Paths of the Warrior, Teacher, Healer, and Visionary.* New York: HarperOne, 1993.

Ellsberg, Robert. *Blessed Among Us: Day by Day with Saintly Witnesses.* Collegeville, MN: Liturgical Press, 2016.

Kidder, Annemarie S., ed. *Essential Writings: Etty Hillesum.* New York: Orbis Books, 2009.

Fleming, Patrick. "From Joplin to Boston: The Spiritual Trauma of Public Tragedy." *America* (July–August 2013), 15–17.

Halifax, Joan. *Standing at the Edge: Finding Freedom Where Fear and Courage Meet.* New York: Flatiron Books, 2019.

Powers, Jessica. "The Garments of God." In *The Selected Poetry of Jessica Powers.* Washington, DC: ICS Publications, 1999.

Wicks, Robert. *Crossing the Desert: Learning to Let Go, See Clearly, and Live Simply.* Notre Dame, IN: Ave Maria Press, 2008.

November

Chittister, Joan. *The Story of Ruth: Twelve Moments in Every Woman's Life.* Grand Rapids: Eerdmans, 2007.

Dickinson, Emily. Quoted in "After Life." *Spirituality and Practice.* www.spiritualityandpractice.com/films/reviews/view/1570.

Gurdjieff, G. I. *In Search of Being: The Fourth Way to Consciousness.* Berkeley: Shambhala, 2021.

Helminski, Kabir. *Living Presence: A Sufi Way to Mindfulness & the Essential Self.* New York: TarcherPerigee, 1992.

Hogan, Linda. *The Woman Who Watches Over the World: A Native Memoir.* New York: W. W. Norton, 2002.

Lachman, Barbara, ed. *The Journal of Hildegard of Bingen.* New York: Harmony, 1993.

Ostaseski, Frank. *The Five Invitations: Discovering What Death Can Teach Us About Living Fully.* New York: Flatiron Books, 2019.

Rupp, Joyce. *The Cup of Our Life: A Guide to Spiritual Growth.* Notre Dame, IN: Ave Maria Press, 2012.

Shields, Mark. *PBS Newshour.* December 18, 2020. www.youtube.com/watch?v=a1MKG_3jC9g.

Steindl-Rast, David. "Giving Thanks for All the Little (and Big) Things in Life," https://gratefulness.org/resource/giving-thanks-big-little.

Tolle, Eckhard. *A New Earth: Awakening to Your Life's Purpose.* New York: Penguin, 2008.

Wiederkehr, Macrina. *Gold in Your Memories: Sacred Moments, Glimpses of God.* Notre Dame, IN: Ave Maria Press, 1998.

December

Children and Family Urban Ministries. Permission given by C. L. Zeitler to use the story.

Holiday, Ryan. *Stillness Is the Key.* New York: Portfolio, 2019.

Ingram, Catherine. *Passionate Presence: Experiencing the Seven Qualities of Awakened Awareness.* Portland, OR: Diamond Books, 2008.

Lacey, Marilyn. *This Flowing Toward Me: A Story of God Arriving in Strangers.* Notre Dame, IN: Ave Maria Press, 2009.

Linner, Rachelle. "This Is Not Play." *Give Us This Day* (December 11, 2020), 118.

Luke, Helen. *Such Stuff as Dreams Are Made On: The Autobiography and Journals of Helen M. Luke.* New York: Harmony/Bell Tower, 2001.

Nerney, Catherine T. *The Compassion Connection: Recovering Our Original Oneness.* New York: Orbis Books, 2018.

Palmer, Parker. *On the Brink of Everything: Grace, Gravity, and Getting Old.* San Francisco: Berrett-Koehler Publishers, 2018.

Richardson, Jan. *Night Visions: Searching the Shadows of Advent and Christmas.* Orlando: Wanton Gospeller Press, 2010.

Wright, Terrence C. *Dorothy Day: An Introduction to Her Life and Thought.* San Francisco: Ignatius Press, 2018.